RPCNA

We gratefully acknowledge our gratitude to the
Faculty of Westminster Theological Seminary,
Philadelphia, Pa. for permission to use
Mr. Spear's Master's Thesis in the
preparation of this book.

introduction

A. The Need For Such A Study

This thesis attempts to present a balanced theological discussion of Christian prayer. The need for such a discussion arises from the importance of prayer for the Christian faith, from the intellectual difficulties posed by prayer, and from the nature of the theological treatment which has been given prayer.

That prayer has occupied an important place in Christian teaching and practice will not be denied by anyone with even a superficial acquaintance with the history of Christianity. Groups of Christians have at times, by choice or necessity, been without an ordained ministry, without the preaching of the Word, without sacraments, singing, or sanctuary. But it may safely be said that whenever Christians have assembled for worship, prayer has been made.

Even as prayer has been an indispensable element of the corporate life of the Church, it has also been regarded as a necessary part of individual piety. One of the first evidences of the conversion of Saul of Tarsus was that he was praying (Acts 9:11). At least in the days before the advocacy of a "religionless Christianity," there would have been almost universal assent to the judgment of Charles Hodge, that "A prayerless Christian and a pulseless man are alike impossible."[1]

The importance of prayer has been reflected in, and in turn enhanced by, the Church's teaching. The great minds of the early Church, men like Origen, Tertullian, Gregory of Nyssa, Cyprian, Theodore of Mopsuestia, and Augustine, wrote about prayer, mainly by means of commentaries on the Lord's Prayer.[2] In the Reformation Era, Luther in his Small Catechism and Calvin in the Institutes of the Christian Religion gave instruction in prayer by means of expositions of the Lord's Prayer. In the Reformed tradition, this instructional emphasis has been carried on in the Heidelberg and Westminster catechisms.

The prominence of prayer in the life of the Church and of individual Christians is a reflection of the place given to prayer in the Scriptures. An indication of the extent of Biblical data will be given in later chapters of this thesis. The evidence justifies the conclusion that prayer fulfills an important function in the accomplishment of the redemptive purpose of God.

The theological discussion of prayer is justified, not only by the importance of the subject, but by its difficulty. The intellectual problems posed by prayer arise primarily from the standpoint of unbelief of the teaching of Scripture. For the most part, unbelief questions the value of prayer, either because it denies the existence of a God to whom meaningful address can be made, or else it conceives the world in such a way that events cannot be ascribed to the activity of a transcendent God.

When difficulties of this kind are raised, the vindication of prayer is inseparably connected with the vindication of the Christian faith. Ménégoz was undoubtedly correct when he wrote, "The problem of prayer: that is the critical issue. There the most desperate conflicts between the friends and foes of religion are being fought and will be fought. And the attitude which theology takes toward this issue will determine in large degree the future of Christianity in the world."[3]

Other problems regarding prayer are posed by the effort to harmonize the Scriptural teaching about prayer with other Scriptural doctrines, such as those of the sovereignty, omniscience, and love of God. If God has infallibly decreed from all eternity whatever comes to pass, if he already knows the needs of his people, and if he extends to them his fatherly care, then how can prayer, petitionary prayer, at least, be meaningful?

Difficulties may arise because of the teaching about prayer which comes from leaders who can point to certain remarkable "answers to prayer," whose personal experience in prayer is impressive, but whose theological foundation is faulty. For example, the writings of S. D. Gordon had wide circulation among evangelicals of an earlier generation. Yet in his book on prayer,[4] he regards Satan as sovereign over the earth, possessing "The kingship of its life, the control and mastery of its forces . . . ."[5] In the face of this usurpation of sovereignty, God does the best he can to regain control, but he is dependent upon man and man's praying. "The results He longs for are being held back, and made smaller because so many of us have not learned how to pray . . . ."[6] Here the roles of petitioner and granter seem almost reversed as God waits upon man's will. Such false theology leads to improper prayer, and requires a careful exposition of the Biblical teaching about prayer for its correction.[7]

The need for the theological discussion of prayer also exists because of the nature of the theological treatment which has been given to prayer within the Reformed tradition.

It has already been noted that Calvin included a discussion of prayer in the Institutes.[8] His doctrine of prayer can scarcely be surpassed for its comprehensiveness, astuteness, and devotional warmth. It appears to require correction only at minor points.[9] It does not, of course, take into account the developments in thought in the last four centuries, and therefore contemporary work is needed.

Calvin treated prayer as the expression of faith, not as a means of grace. Continental theologians followed his example in the enumeration of the means of grace, with the result that prayer was all but eliminated as a topic within the system of theology. Thus, no section on prayer will be found in Heppe's compendium of Reformed theological works.[10] Modern Reformed theologians, such as H. Bavinck, Berkhof, Berkouwer and Hoeksema, true to the continental Reformed tradition, fail to accord any separate discussion to prayer.

In the development of British Reformed theology, prayer came to be regarded as one of the means of grace. The Westminster standards display some ambivalence in this regard, in that the Confession of Faith discusses prayer under the heading "Of Religious Worship, and the Sabbath Day," while the Larger Catechism and Shorter Catechism list prayer as one of the "outward and ordinary means" by which the benefits of redemption are communicated.[11] Systematic theology in Britain and America often followed the outline of the Catechisms, and so prayer will be found as a topic of theology in such works as Dick's Lectures on Theology[12] and Hodge's Systematic Theology.[13] Dick's discussion is full and helpful; Hodge's is less so, being occupied primarily with refuting objections to prayer raised by the scientific determinism which was popular in the nineteenth century. These works, however, are a century old. There has been almost no comprehensive theological treatment of prayer from a Reformed standpoint since the time of Hodge. Abraham Kuyper's discussion,[14] like the earlier one of John Owen,[15] is limited by the special attention given to the role of the Holy Spirit in prayer.

Contemporary discussions of prayer, even those which have

come from allegedly Reformed circles, are characterized by the abandonment of Biblical views of God and the world.[16] While the attempt is made to salvage some meaning for prayer, the result is a virtual abandonment of prayer as it is presented in the Scriptures.

B.   The Theological Standpoint

This study of prayer is intended to be normative rather than descriptive; that is, it seeks to show what Christian prayer ought to be and can be, not merely to determine how Christians through the years have actually understood and practiced prayer.

This purpose makes it mandatory to adopt a criterion in relation to which the norms for prayer may be established. The criterion which is adopted here as dependable and authoritative is the teaching of the Scriptures of the Old and New Testaments, regarded as inspired by God and therefore inerrant.

To give a full justification for such a standpoint lies outside the scope of the thesis; if it were given, it would follow the views expressed by Abraham Kuyper regarding the fundamental, regulative principle of theology.[17] It may be said here, however, that in presenting a theology of Christian prayer it is believed to be necessary to follow the teaching of Jesus Christ regarding both prayer and the ultimate criterion of truth. Confidence in Scripture rests on Christ's attestation to the validity of the Old Testament (for example, in John 10:35), and on his promise to send the Holy Spirit to guide his apostles into all truth (John 16:13).

The investigation takes place within the tradition of Reformed theology. This involves a consciousness of a history of theological discussion, in which certain questions regarding prayer have been deemed important. It involves a special sensitivity to the matter of God's sovereignty. It involves a certain way of approaching Scripture, in which the meaning is sought through study of terms and grammatical structure, and in which there is an awareness of both the unity and the historical progression of God's revelation. The Reformed standpoint is itself subject to correction by Scripture; but it has been consciously adopted because it is believed to be the viewpoint which the Scripture sets forth.

C.   The Plan of the Thesis

Scripture nowhere presents a unified, concise discussion of prayer. Instead, the data is to be found in literally hundreds of references to prayer scattered throughout both Testaments. To collect these references it is necessary to have in mind a preliminary definition of prayer, so that one will recognize a reference to prayer in Scripture even if the usual words for prayer are not used. Such a definition is given, and the method by which it was formulated is described, in the first chapter of the thesis.

While primary attention is given in the thesis to the New Testament teaching on prayer, the Old Testament background is constantly in view. The most important elements of that background are presented in Chapter II.

The bulk of the Biblical data is so great that attention cannot be given in the thesis to every Biblical reference to prayer. The selection of passages to be discussed involves reflection on the Biblical material to determine elements of the teaching which receive special emphasis in Scripture, and those which appear to require clarification. This reflection also involves the attempt to correlate the various aspects of the doctrine, and in this attempt certain problems arise which require discussion.

Along with reflection on the Biblical data it is necessary to note how theologians and the confessional statements of the Church have handled the subject of prayer. As theological treatment and Biblical material are considered together, the topics which warrant attention emerge, and it is seen that they may be divided into those relating to the objective conditions of prayer, having to do with the nature and activity of God in his relation to the world, and those relating to prayer in its subjective aspects, having to do with the state and activity of the one who prays. The Biblical passages which are to be discussed are accordingly arranged in this order.

The objective aspects of prayer are discussed in the third, fourth, and fifth chapters of the thesis, in which it will be noted that the subject matter is divided along Trinitarian lines. This method of procedure not only has the benefit of long historical precedent (the Apostles' Creed and Calvin's Institutes are so organized); but the Biblical material itself warrants such a division. As will be seen, Scripture itself refers to distinctive roles of the Father, Son and Spirit in relation to prayer.

Chapters VI and VII deal with prayer in its subjective aspects, having to do, respectively, with the qualities required in the one who would pray acceptably, and with the content of proper prayer.

The body of the thesis is mainly occupied with exegesis; a theological work requires, however, that the findings of the exegetical study be brought together in a unified, balanced statement of what may be known on a certain subject. This is the purpose of the eighth chapter, which seeks to give a concise, Biblical statement regarding prayer, based on the exegesis which has been set forth.

The Biblical teaching about prayer gives rise to certain objections, both from without and from within the circle of faith. From the side of faith, the necessity of prayer is, tacitly at least, apt to be questioned. Skepticism denies the efficacy of prayer, or else seeks a "natural" explanation for it. The ninth chapter is occupied with the defense of prayer against these objections.

chapter 1

the definition of prayer

When one approaches the Bible to discover what it teaches about prayer, he must already have some notion of what prayer is, otherwise he will not recognize those passages in which information about prayer is given. He is familiar with a human activity which is called prayer; as he reads Scripture, he finds the same kind of activity being referred to. By studying such references, his preliminary understanding of prayer may be corrected and enlarged; but without that preliminary understanding he could not begin at all. It is therefore necessary at the beginning of this study to delineate the subject which is under discussion by giving a provisional definition of the concept of prayer.

Prayer, as it is understood here, is human speech that is addressed to God.

It is a human activity that is under consideration. The thesis does not attempt to determine whether angels, for example, or animals, are capable of prayer. These questions might be valid and interesting, but it is not the purpose of this thesis to enter into them.

Prayer is here regarded as speech; that is, it is a form of expression which is potentially formulatable into words. Prayer is thus distinguished on one hand from mere mental activity, such as meditation; on the other, it is distinguished from bodily activity which is not translatable into verbal content. Obviously, it is not always possible to determine where the border between meditation and silent prayer lies, or to distinguish between a gesture which may be a kind of language and one that is not.

It may be said that meditation is a form of prayer, or that acts of charity are essentially prayers; no doubt instances of the use of the word "prayer" in such ways could be cited. Certainly Scripture encourages both meditation and Christian service. But the words used to describe speech addressed to God are not applied in the Bible to these activities, and this indicates that, whatever may be said about meditation and activity, prayer as a lingual act may be investigated separately.

By denoting prayer as a lingual act, it is not meant that it must be primarily an act of the intellect. Speech expresses emotion: a cry for help, an exclamation of joy, a gesture of love, are truly forms of language.

Prayer as it is discussed here is further defined as speech addressed to God. The English word "pray" is often used, of course, to denote a request made by one man upon another, and many examples of this kind of "prayer" are found in Scripture. But there are essential differences between prayer on a human level and prayer which ascends from man to God. It is with the latter that this study is concerned.[1]

When prayer is defined as speech addressed to God, it is evident that many kinds of speech may be included. When man is confronted with the majesty and perfection of God, his proper response is adoration; "Thine, O Lord, is the greatness, and the power, and the glory, and the victory, and the majesty . . ." (I Chron. 29:11)[2]. When he reflects upon the blessings which God has given, he gives thanks: "O give thanks to the Lord, for he is good, for his stedfast love endures for ever" (Ps. 136:1). Faced with the holiness of God and awareness of his own sinfulness, man's prayer is one of confession: "Against thee, thee only, have I sinned, and done that which is evil in thy sight . . ." (Ps. 51:4). Awareness of the sovereignty and the goodness of God leads to the prayer of submission: "Into thy hand I commit my spirit; thou hast redeemed me, O Lord, faithful God" (Ps. 31:5). Love for God and confidence in his grace produce promises of future obedience: "Then we will never turn back from thee; give us life, and we will call on thy name!" (Ps. 80:18). A sense of need, a desire for the fulness of God's blessing, gives rise to petition: "O Lord, hear; O Lord, forgive; O Lord, give heed and act; delay not, for thy own sake, O my God . . ." (Dan. 9:19).[3]

Of all of these forms of prayer, adoration, thanksgiving, confession, submission, commitment, and petition, the last is most important from a theological standpoint. This is so not only because of the prominence given to petition in the Lord's Prayer, but also because most of the questions regarding prayer are connected with petition. Both the question of the proper content of prayer and that of answers to prayer relate primarily to petition. Therefore the discussion of the theology of prayer will give special attention to the matter of petitionary prayer. At the same time, it must be recognized that prayer is not limited to petition, and the thesis attempts to deal with the other aspects of prayer as well.

chapter II

the old testament background

A consistently Reformed view of Scripture involves both a recognition of the inspired character of Scripture taken as a whole and also an awareness of the progressive nature of revelation.[1] All the books of the Bible are authoritative and trustworthy; but a distinction must be made between revelation which is incomplete and preparatory, and that which is full and final.

In the Bible itself, the Old and New Testaments bear the stamp, respectively, of preparation and fulfillment. As the embodiment of the revelation given with the advent of the Messiah, the New Testament possesses a finality which is not claimed by the Old Testament. Thus the contrast: "For the law was given through Moses; grace and truth came through Jesus Christ" (John 1:17). "In many and various ways God spoke of old to our fathers by the prophets; but in these last days he has spoken to us by a Son . . ." (Heb. 1:1,2). Because of this, the New Testament stands in the foreground and the Old Testament in the background of theological investigation. With regard to prayer, the New Testament provides knowledge not given in the Old Testament, especially with regard to the roles of Jesus Christ and the Holy Spirit in prayer. Further, in the light of the New Testament it is seen that some aspects of the practice of prayer in the Old, for example the connection between prayer and the sacrificial system, had only a temporary and typical significance, and are now superceded.

This does not mean that the Old Testament material can be ignored in building a theology of prayer. The New Testament teaching constantly assumes knowledge of what has gone before, and cannot be properly understood without it.

It is for that reason that attention must be given to some of the significant aspects of the teaching about prayer in the Old Testament. No attempt is made to present a full picture of the Old Testament theory and practice of prayer.[2] The topics for discussion have been chosen because of their importance for understanding the New Testament data.

A.   General Characteristics of the Material

It is permissible to speak of the doctrine of prayer in the Old Testament in the sense that a "doctrine" may be developed from what is only implicit in the literature of the Old Testament. There is a relatively small amount of positive teaching about prayer, found mostly in the wisdom literature, the Psalms, and the prophetic books; and a much larger amount of descriptive material, in which there is recorded the occurrence and content of actual prayer.

A didactic statement about prayer in the Old Testament requires careful weighing, since it is often difficult to determine whether such a statement represents an inspired (and therefore authoritative) utterance about prayer, or is an inspired record of fallable human reasoning about prayer, such as occurs in the book of Job (Job 8:5,6 with 42:7). The historical accounts of prayer also require careful attention to the context and to the whole of the Biblical teaching in order to determine which examples are meant to be normative, and which merely give an accurate portrayal of improper prayer.

B.   The Nature of Old Testament Prayer

Prayer stands in the Old Testament as an integral part of a loving, trusting, reverent relationship with God. That is to say, prayer is not regarded only as a "duty" which a pious man should perform; rather it is the manifestation in speech of the religious consciousness of the believer. It is not just a part of piety, but piety itself come to expression.

That prayer is inseparable from the religious life is indicated in a number of ways in the Old Testament. It appears from the lack of any record of the instituting of prayer, such as we have for marriage (Gen. 2:23,24) and the Sabbath (Gen. 2:2,3). When the Law was given at Sinai, there was both ratification of previously given revelation, and a new revelation of the will of God. Yet in that Law, the only explicit instruction regarding prayer is that which concerns confession of sin (Lev. 5:5; 16:21; 26:40-42). The instruction about prayer which is given in the poetical and prophetic portions of the Old Testament deals with the proper ways in which prayer should be made. That godly men will pray is assumed; it is only necessary that they be instructed how to pray aright.

In the Old Testament, then, prayer is not treated as a part of the law, as a duty imposed upon men. Rather, prayer arises spontaneously from the man who is conscious of his need and of God's power and goodness.

When men "say prayers" instead of praying, when there is a separation between prayer and life, then prayer is meaningless. When God sees that people " . . . draw near with their mouth, and honor me with their lips, while their hearts are far from me, and their fear of me is a commandment learned by rote . . ." (Isa. 29:13), then he promises judgment.

Prayer in the Old Testament is the expression of the religious consciousness of a man who does not exist in and of himself, but who stands in Covenant relation with the living God. Prayer is not a soliloquy, nor is it a magical incantation; it is intercourse with the God who has revealed himself by his word and in mighty acts of redemption toward his people. Prayer presupposes a God who hears (Ps. 65:2); who is in control of all the events of history (Isa. 44:24-45:8); who does not act arbitrarily, but in accordance with his own nature (Gen. 18:25) and in fulfillment of his promise (Ps. 105:8-11); and who has promised to respond to the prayers of his people (II Chron. 7:14,15). Prayer which rests on such assumptions is not a late development in the Old Testament, but is present from the Patriarchal Age forward.[3] It is impossible to discern in the Old Testament an evolutionary development from a "primitive" to a more sophisticated practice of prayer.[4]

C.   The Content of Old Testament Petition

The content of prayer in the Old Testament is of special interest because in the view of many it exhibits not only the incompleteness which is due to its early place in the history of redemption and revelation, but also has characteristics which are improper and require correction in the light of New Testament revelation.[5] Naturally, the range of content is very great; but when the question is asked, "For what did Old Testament believers ask, or thank God?" the answer can be expressed in a very few major categories.

First of all, there is prayer for divine guidance. One of the earliest recorded prayers, that of Abraham's servant Eliezer, is such a prayer (Gen. 24:12-14). The seeking of direction from God occurs with great frequency throughout the Old Testament, finding embodiment in Israel's Psalmody: "Teach me the way that I should go, for to thee I lift up my soul" (Ps. 143:8).

Prayer for provision is another recurrent theme: "Some wandered in desert wastes . . . hungry and thirsty, their soul fainted within them. Then they cried to the Lord in their trouble, and he delivered them from their distress . . ." (Ps. 107:4-6). The reference in this Psalm is to the Exodus; repeatedly, Israel prayed for provision of water and food, and the prayers were heard.

There is also prayer for deliverance from disease, and from such natural dangers as storms at sea. Hezekiah was granted an additional fifteen years of life in response to such a prayer (II Kings 20:1-6). On the other hand, Asa is criticized for failing to seek the Lord with regard to his disease (II Chron. 16:12).

In the face of the uncertainty of the future, of the need for food and shelter, of the threat of disease and natural disaster, the Old Testament believer sought for God's help in prayer. But more prominent than all these, in the Old Testament, is prayer for deliverance from enemies—and for their destruction. This is strikingly expressed in the words of Moses which marked Israel's journey through the wilderness: "And whenever the ark set out, Moses said, 'Arise, O Lord, and let thy enemies be scattered; and let them that hate thee flee before thee.' And when it rested, he said, 'Return, O Lord, to the ten thousand thousands of Israel' " (Num. 10:35-36). The Psalms are filled with passages in which pleas for God's mercies are inseparably linked with petitions for the pouring out of his wrath upon the enemies of the Psalmist and of Israel.

From factors such as these, it would not be difficult to construct a view of Old Testament prayer which would regard it as materialistic, selfish, unspiritual—as an effort to manipulate God to the advantage of an individual, or of a nation greedy for conquest. And it is not to be denied that individuals in the Old Testament, and Israel itself, at times fell short of the proper understanding of their relationship to God, or of the purpose of prayer.

Nevertheless, to brand Old Testament prayer generally as unchristian, is to ignore a number of relevant considerations.

There is, first of all, much prayer in the Old Testament which does not refer primarily to temporal benefits, but to the favor of God as such. There is a rich strand of prayer in the Psalter in which the possession of God's favor is recognized as surpassing all other goods: "Because thy stedfast love is better than life, my lips will praise thee" (Ps. 63:3). Perplexity over the prosperity of the wicked finds its solution in recognition of the supreme value of fellowship with God (Ps. 73; Hab. 3:17-19). It is this desire for God's favor which leads to the prayer of penitence which is so prominent throughout the Old Testament: "Cast me not away from thy presence, and take not thy holy Spirit from me. Restore to me the joy of thy salvation, and uphold me with a willing spirit" (Ps. 51: 11,12).

The presence of this aspect of prayer in the Old Testament makes it possible to place prayer for mundane blessings in proper perspective. For, in its better moments, at least, Israel regarded temporal blessings as the manifestation of God's favor. Famine, pestilence, oppression by enemies, were all instruments of God to chasten his people for their sin. Prayer for relief from these calamities was therefore at the same time prayer for forgiveness and the restoration of God's favor. Periods of short-lived repentance, as for instance during the time of the Judges, indicated that at times escape from temporal misery was the prime motivation for prayer. But certainly there are other instances when it was primarily the the renewal of God's favor which was sought, and temporal deliverance was desired only as an evidence of restored fellowship (cf. Ps. 42 and 43).

Beyond this, it must be recognized that because Israel was a nation chosen by the Lord to have a special role in the fulfillment of his purpose of redemption, the enemies of Isarel were at the same time the enemies of God. Even the plea of an individual for vengeance must be understood in this regard, for he is a member of the Covenant people (and in the case of a number of the imprecatory Psalms, stands at their head as king). Imprecations in the Old Testament need not be regarded as expressions of personal hatred; they express a desire for the glorification of God in the success of his purposes and in the defeat of his enemies.[6]

It may be said, then, that the content of Old Testament prayer is not limited to a desire for temporal welfare; but there is a deeper quest for the enjoyment of God's favor both in this life and beyond, and a desire that God may be glorified in the accomplishment of his purpose in the world.

D.   Prayer and Sacrifice

The relation between sacrifice and prayer in the Old Testament is of interest not only for a correct understanding of Old Testament piety, but because it gives the necessary background for understanding the relation between the work of Christ and prayer.[7]

The relation has sometimes been regarded as that between

"earlier" and "later" or between "lower" and "higher." Herrmann, for example, sees in the Psalms the reflection of " . . . a piety in which the prayer or song of thanksgiving has taken the place of sacrifice."[8] The implication is present that the sacrificial system was basically in conflict with the more "spiritual" religion of the Psalter, and had no essential value for genuine piety.

It must certainly be acknowledged that in the Old Testament there was no rigid rule that prayer must always be accompanied by sacrifice. Examples of prayer without specific mention of sacrifice occur in early times (Gen. 24:12-14; 32:9-12), after the giving of the Law (Num. 14:13-19), and of course, during the Captivity, when no sacrifices could be offered at all (Dan. 9:3-19). It is proper to assume that, while the Scripture records only central events in the history of Israel, there was a continual practice of personal and family devotion which could not be directly connected with the ceremonies of the sanctuary. When the Psalmist speaks of praying three times a day (Ps. 55:17), it is not to be supposed that he went to the sanctuary to offer sacrifice that often.

It would be unjustified, however, to conclude that there was no essential relationship between prayer and sacrifice in the Old Testament. Rather, the evidence suggests that the sanctuary and its sacrifices were seldom absent from the mind of the Israelite when he prayed.

Prayer and sacrifice occur in conjunction when it is said that Abraham " . . . built an altar to the Lord and called on the name of the Lord" (Gen. 12:8). Job prayed for his friends as they offered their sacrifices (Job 42:8,9). In the Mosaic ceremony, confession of sin accompanied the sin-offering (Lev. 5:5; 16:21), and David made provision for congregational singing, which is a form of prayer, in connection with the sacrificial ritual (I Chron. 16). Songs of thanksgiving were sung as sacrifices were offered at the dedication of the restored wall of Jerusalem (Neh. 12:31-43).

During times of exile from Jerusalem, the sanctuary remained precious to God's people (cf. Ps. 42 and 43). Daniel's custom of praying with his window open toward Jerusalem (Dan. 6:10) is an indication of the linking of prayer and the place of sacrifice. Undoubtedly Solomon's prayer at the dedication of the Temple was the basis for Daniel's practice: " . . . if they repent with all their mind and with all their heart in the land of their captivity . . . and pray toward their land . . . and the house which I have built for thy name, then hear thou from heaven thy dwelling place their prayer . . ." (II Chron. 6:38,39). Prayer was to be directed toward the Temple, not because God was located there (cf. II Chron. 6:18), but because it was the place of sacrifice: "Then the Lord appeared to Solomon in the night and said to him, 'I have heard your prayer, and have chosen this place for myself as a house of sacrifice' " (II Chron. 7:12).

Daniel could pray, even though no sacrifices were then being offered; but he prayed with the memory of the sacrificial ritual of the Temple in his mind. This suggests a conclusion which the later study of the New Testament will confirm: that prayer in the Old Testament did not depend upon animal sacrifices for its efficacy; but that the sacrificial system was instituted by God to teach his people that as sinners they could approach him only by way of an atonement.

Beyond this, it may be said that even when prayer is apparently set over against sacrifice, as in Psalms 50 and 51, it is not necessary to interpret this as a replacement of sacrifice by prayer. Rather, what is being condemned is the formal offering of sacrifice without the appropriate attitude of heart. Where there is no contrition, then God "has no delight in sacrifice." But when there has been repentance and the restoration of God's favor, then God will "delight in right sacrifices, in burnt offerings and whole burnt offerings" (Ps. 51:16-19).

Thus prayer and sacrifice in the Old Testament were not contradictory, but complementary. Sacrifice was not an erroneous way of approaching God, but actually set forth the only way in which sinful men could approach a holy God, namely, by way of the shedding of blood. Whether he prayed at the sanctuary or in Babylon, the believing Israelite was conscious of his need of a covering for his sin and so prayed depending upon the promise of a Saviour who was yet to come and who was typified in the ritual of the sanctuary.

E.   Intercession in the Old Testament

The ceremonial ritual of the Old Testament set forth not only the need for atonement in approaching God, but also the need for an intercessor.

The role of intercessor in the patriarchal age was performed by the head of the family (see Job 1:5). Under the Mosaic Law, a hereditary priesthood was established, by whom sacrifices were ordinarily to be offered (Ex. 28,29). The clearest indication of the priest's role as intercessor was seen in the burning of incense upon the golden altar (Ex. 30:1-10). The incense was the symbol of prayer ascending to God (cf. Ps. 141:2; Rev. 5:8); it was burned morning and evening by the priests, as " . . . a perpetual incense before the Lord" (Ex. 30:8). The pious Israelite, as he prayed in his dwelling, would remember that in the sanctuary the priest was burning incense before the Lord in his behalf; and so there was presented to his mind the concept of an intercessor, of prayer being made continually on his behalf.

But the figure of an intercessor is not only found in the ceremonies of the Old Testament. The history of the Covenant people was itself a preparatory revelation which looked forward to the coming of the Messiah.[9] And in the history of Israel there is a recurrence of a function of intercession performed by one who stands at the head of God's people.

Thus Abraham intercedes with God for the righteous who are threatened with destruction in Sodom (Gen. 18:22-32). Moses, as the leader of the children of Israel, over and over again prays for provision and for mercy in behalf of his people (Ex. 15:25; 17:4; 32:11-14; 34:8,9, etc.). Israel is so dependent upon Samuel's prayers that even when they refuse to be ruled by God through him, they seek his intercession for them (I Sam. 12:19,23). David and Solomon, as rulers, utter memorable prayers for their people (I Chron. 29:10-19; II Chron. 6:12-42). In times of revival, Asa, Jehoshaphat and Hezekiah intercede with the Lord in behalf of Israel (II Chron. 14:11; 20:5-12; 30:18-20). During and after the Exile, Daniel and Ezra appear as leaders who make intercession for the remnant (Dan. 9:3-19; Ezra 9:5-15).

From this long tradition of the ruler who was also intercessor, then, Isaiah's prophecy regarding the Suffering Servant, who was to make intercession for transgressors (Isa. 53:12) would be understood. And the New Testament references to Christ's intercession are to be seen against this background.

chapter III

the object of prayer

With this chapter begins the theological consideration of the objective conditions of prayer. "Objective" is used in this context to refer to the state of affairs which exists independently of the condition and activity of the one who prays. Prayer, in the Bible, is not viewed as a purely subjective phenomenon. Prayer has an objective Referrent; it is addressed to God. Prayer is seen not as purely human activity, but as the result also of the prior activity of God. Prayer, in its petitionary aspect, anticipates results which are regarded as being attributable to divine action. Prayer is thus seen to have its basis in the nature and activity of God, and is meaningful only because of that basis. It is for this reason that a discussion of the objective conditions of prayer must precede the discussion of prayer in its subjective aspects.

A.   The Assumptions About God Which Underlie Prayer

When prayer was defined earlier as speech addressed to God,[1] the definition was a preliminary one, used only to indicate the field of investigation. An examination of the Biblical passages which refer to prayer shows that prayer is distinguished from other speech just because it is addressed to God. Thus, while a plea for help or forgiveness might be directed to another man as well as to God, and might even use the same words, the two kinds of petition are quite different. This is so because prayer to God, if it stems from faith, takes into account what is revealed to man of God's nature. What difference this makes will appear from a discussion of the attributes of God which are of the most direct importance for prayer.

1.   Omniscience

A plea addressed to men depends upon factors of space and time in order to be heard—response can come only from one who can be reached by sound waves, or to whom a message can be sent by physical means. There are limitations of language; a plea for help might be disregarded because it was received by men of a different tongue, or those who could not read.

Prayer to God is distinguished from speech to men because it does not have such limitation. Prayer presupposes the ability of God to hear and understand, no matter what language is spoken, or what the circumstances are in which it is made. Christian prayer relies upon the omniscience of God.

The Psalmist was confident of God's ability to hear, even though he prayed "from the end of the earth" (Ps. 61:2). At the dedication of the Temple, Solomon recognized that God could not be localized in any place of worship, but that he would hear prayer from heaven (II Chron. 6:18,21). Thus prayer would be heard even from the battlefield, or from the land of captivity (II Chron. 6:34,38). Elijah's ironic advice to the prophets of Baal to pray loudly, since their god might be at a distance, or preoccupied, or asleep (I Kings 18:27), carries with it the implied assertion that it would be absurd to attribute such things to the living God, the one who " . . . will neither slumber nor sleep" (Ps. 121:4).

Jesus related the omniscience of God to prayer when he taught that men should pray privately to their Father "who sees in secret" (Matt. 6:6). The quiet prayer of the closet does not escape the notice of God.

The omniscience of God is important for prayer, not only because it gives assurance that prayer is heard, but because it points up the necessity of sincerity in prayer. Since " . . . before him no creature is hidden, but all are open and laid bare to the eyes of him with whom we have to do" (Heb. 4:13), there is no possibility that mere words, the formal act of praying, will induce a favorable response from God. It is because God is omniscient, according to Jesus' teaching, that the "heaping up of empty phrases," characteristic of the prayers of Gentiles, is of no avail (Matt. 6:7,8).

2.   Omnipotence

Prayer to God is further distinguished from speech addressed to men in that it regards the power of its hearer as unlimited.

The contrast between the help to be expected from finite man, even the most powerful, and from the infinite God, is strikingly expressed by the Psalmist: "Put not your trust in princes, in a son of man, in whom there is no help. When his breath departs he returns to the earth; on that very day his plans perish. Happy is he whose help is the God of Jacob . . . who made heaven and earth . . . who keeps faith for ever" (Ps. 146:3-6).

The prayer of faith is addressed to God, who " . . . is able to do far more abundantly than all we ask or think" (Eph. 3:20). It is instructive to note what is recorded of Zechariah, the father of John the Baptist (Luke 1:11-20). The angel who came to announce John's impending birth informed Zechariah that his prayer for a son was heard. Yet, because he and Elizabeth had now passed the age of fertility, Zechariah did not believe the message from God. As a result, he was struck dumb until the birth should occur. And the birth of John was to give evidence of the fact that " . . . with God nothing will be impossible" (Luke 1:37). The conclusion is to be drawn that prayer which places limits upon the ability of God falls short of the standard which is set in Scripture.[2]

3.   Sovereignty

The distinctiveness of prayer to God lies not only in that it contemplates the infinite ability of God in contrast to the limited ability of man; the distinction arises also from the kind of activity in the world which is attributed to God. Prayer to God recognizes him as the ultimate cause of all events, while men have only a secondary and limited role in the occurrence of particular events. Omnipotence is not seen as sheer potential, but as a power actively at work in the world.[3] That is to say, prayer, according to the Bible, is based upon a belief in the providential control of God over the world.

Apart from a belief in providence, prayer would be limited to adoration, worshipping God for what he is in himself, and for his wisdom and bounty as shown in the original creation of the world. Yet everywhere in Scripture are prayers of thanksgiving for God's wonderful works in history, and petitions for his gracious activity in the near and distant future.

The evidence is so abundant that only a few examples need to be cited. David's prayer in designating Solomon to succeed him includes a recognition of God's providence: "Thine, O Lord, is the greatness, and the power, and the glory, and the victory, and the majesty; for all that is in the heaven and in the earth is thine; thine is the kingdom, O Lord, and thou art exalted as head above all. Both riches and honor come from thee, and thou rulest over all . . . And now we thank thee, our God, and praise thy glorious name" (I Chron. 29:11-13).

Nebuchadnezzar was taught to recognize God's sovereignty even over rulers by seven years of madness, and upon his restoration he praised God, for " . . . he does according to his will in the host of heaven and among the inhabitants of the earth; and none can stay his hand or say to him, 'What doest thou?' " (Dan. 4:35).

That God's control extends over all events is indicated not only by the exhortation to give thanks in all circumstances (I Thess. 5:18), but by the range of petition. Prayer recognizes God as the giver of daily sustenance (Matt. 6:30-33); as the source of orderly government and peaceful society (I Tim. 2:1,2); as the controller of circumstances which would permit a journey (Rom. 1:9,10); as the cause of the sanctification of believers (Phil. 1:9-11). Thus it is assumed that events in the natural world, conditions of human society, and developments in human personality are all ultimately under the control of God.

The prevalence in Scripture of prayers of thanksgiving and petition, and of commands that such prayers be made, points to a doctrine of providence, which recognizes the hand of God in all events that occur. Those who reject the notion of providence, who maintain that events occur independently of God, must either reject the bulk of Scriptural data on prayer as invalid, or else find a hidden meaning in Biblical prayer, a meaning which is not conveyed by the words that are used.

There is another aspect of the sovereignty of God, besides providence, which is important for prayer. God is sovereign over man, not only by way of the control upon which man is dependent, but in terms of the authority which makes man responsible. That is to say, Biblical prayer acknowledges God as the supreme lawgiver and judge.

A consciousness of the supreme authority of God leads to the prayer of unconditional commitment. A bare belief in God's pervasive control of the world could lead to passive submission; but the prayers of Scripture exhibit more. It is acknowledged that the will of God is not only effective, but good, and the revelation of that will is adopted as the standard for man's life. Thus, in a Psalm which celebrates the power of God in creation, and in determining the affairs of rulers and nations, the moral perfection of God's rule is acknowledged: "For the word of the Lord is upright; and all his work is done in faithfulness. He loves righteousness and justice; the earth is full of the steadfast love of the Lord" (Ps. 33:4,5). In like manner, the recognition that "Our God is in the heavens; he does whatever he pleases" (Ps. 115:3) calls for the placing of trust in him

(Ps. 115:10,11).

The prayer of Jesus in Gethsemane, " . . . thy will be done" (Matt. 26:42), was not a statement of resignation, but of dedication. He came in the spirit attributed to him by the Messianic prophecy, "I delight to do thy will, O my God; thy law is within my heart" (Ps. 40:8). And the petition of the Lord's Prayer, "Thy will be done" (Matt. 6:10), is to be understood in this sense of commitment.

Along with the adoption of God's will as the standard of life and conduct goes the consciousness of failure to do God's will, and hence the prayer for forgiveness of sin: "For thy name's sake, O Lord, pardon my guilt, for it is great" (Ps. 25:11).

This sense of ultimate responsibility to God is another element which distinguishes prayer to God from other human speech. The loyalty pledged to another man must always be subordinate to one's ultimate allegiance to the will of God (Acts 5:29). And while a plea for forgiveness may properly be addressed to another man, yet it is only appropriate if one has at the same time offended God. And the offence against God is recognized as of the greater seriousness. Thus, while David had undoubtedly wronged both Uriah and Bathsheba, he could pray to God, "Against thee, thee only have I sinned, and done that which is evil in thy sight" (Ps. 51:4). Forgiveness, in the final analysis, comes from God.

It may be seen, then, that prayer is a unique form of human speech because of the uniqueness of the one to whom it is addressed. Prayer in the Bible assumes, and often explicitly asserts, that God is omniscient; that his power is unlimited; that he is actively at work in the world, controlling and directing all events; and that he is the one to whom man is finally answerable. Because prayer makes such assumptions, it must be made to God alone. It is included in the worship and service which are to be rendered only to the living God (Matt. 4:10).

These presuppositions lie upon the face of the data on prayer in both the Old and the New Testament. The passages which have been cited are representative passages which reflect characteristics of the material as a whole. That this is the case will scarcely be denied; the point which is contested is whether these assumptions are essential to Biblical prayer and normative in all ages, or whether they are incidental and transitory.[4]

The distinctiveness of prayer addressed to God as compared with speech addressed to men has been emphasized in this discussion.

This has been done in order to lay the groundwork for consideration of two questions which arise as to the proper object of prayer. The first has to do with the invocation of saints; the second, with the doctrine of the Trinity.

B.   The Invocation of Saints

Many of the Reformed Confessions found it necessary to emphasize that prayer is to be made to God alone. For example, the Second Helvetic Confession says, " . . . since we do believe in God alone, we assuredly call upon him alone, and we do so through Christ . . . For this reason we do not adore, worship, or pray to the saints in heaven, or to other gods, and we do not acknowledge them as our intercessors or mediators before the Father in heaven."[5] Statements such as this had chiefly in view the Roman Catholic practices of the invocation and veneration of the saints, and the use of relics and images in worship.

The Catholic Church was sensitive to this charge of idolatry ascribed to such practices, and replied to it at the Council of Trent: " . . . they think impiously who deny that the saints who enjoy eternal happiness in heaven are to be invoked, or who assert that they do not pray for men, or that our invocation of them to pray for each of us individually is idolatry . . ."[6] Strictly speaking, the invocation of saints involved asking for their prayers, not praying to them for direct aid. It was regarded as an extension of the Scripturally approved practice of asking for the prayer support of other Christians.

The Reformers objected to the theory of the invocation and veneration of saints on the grounds that it lacked positive Biblical warrant.[7] But the charge of idolatry was based upon the conviction that in practice, prayers to the saints involved ascribing to them what belongs to God alone. Calvin states his judgement that " . . . there are very many who do not refrain from the horrid sacrilege of calling upon the saints now not as helpers but as determiners of their salvation . . . How much farther has this devilish insolence spread, when men do not hesitate to transfer to the dead what properly belonged to God and Christ?"[8] The Council of Trent as much as acknowledged this in calling for the removal of "all superstition" from the invocation of saints.[9]

The invocation of saints was rightly termed idolatry because by its very nature it blurred the clear distinction between prayer to the Most High and speech addressed to man. The saints in heaven are invisible, out of reach of ordinary human communication. Yet they are presumed to be able, like God, to "hear in heaven." Further, the requirement for beatification, that miracles be worked through prayer to the saint,[10] made it very easy to attribute supernatural power to the saint himself. Events were thought to be under the control of various saints, rather than under the sovereignty of God. As Calvin says, "Then each man adopted a particular saint as a tutelary deity, in whose keeping he put his trust."[11]

Because such abuses are inherent in the invocation of dead saints, the rule must be maintained that prayer is to be made to God alone.

C.   The Doctrine of the Trinity and the Question of the Object of Prayer

Paul Tillich bases, in part, his rejection of the traditional formulation of the doctrine of the Trinity upon the problems which it poses for the practice of prayer:

> "In terms of religious devotion, one can ask, Is the prayer to one of the three personae in whom the one divine substance exists directed toward someone different from another of the three to whom another prayer is directed? If there is no difference, why does one not simply address the prayer to God? If there is a difference, for example, in function, how is tritheism avoided? The concepts of ousia and hypostasis or of substantia and persona do not answer this basic devotional problem. They only confuse it and open the way to the unlimited number of objects of prayer which appeared in connection with the veneration of Mary and the saints - in spite of the theological distinctions between a genuine prayer, directed to God (adoration), and the evocation of the saints."[12]

The assertion which Tillich seems to be making here is that if the object of prayer is simply God, then the distinction of persons in the Godhead cannot be maintained: on the other hand, if prayer is made to one of the persons of the Godhead, the unity of the divine essence cannot be maintained. To this it must be replied, that the Biblical data indicated that prayer may indeed be made to one of the persons of the Godhead in distinction from the others, but that it does not follow that the unity of the Godhead is thereby destroyed. While Tillich finds in the experience of prayer an insuperable difficulty with regard to the doctrine of the Trinity, it is in relation to prayer in the New Testament that some of the clearest evidence for the Trinity is given.

The deity of Christ has always been the crucial question as to the doctrine of the Trinity. Therefore it will be helpful to look first at the teaching of Scripture concerning Christ as the Object of prayer. The full significance of this teaching can be realized only against the background of the principle, reiterated by Christ himself, that God is to be the exclusive Object of worship (Matt. 4:10).

It is apparent that the essential deity of Jesus Christ was not always, perhaps not usually, recognized by those who addressed requests to him during the days of his earthly ministry. Even his miracles did not serve immediately to distinguish him from prophets of the Old Testament, whose ministry had also involved the working of miracles. The technical New Testament word for prayer (*proseuchomai*) is never used of requests made to Jesus while on earth, while the common term for asking *(erōtaō)*, which is almost never used of prayer to the Father, is constantly used of requests made to Jesus.[13] We find the father of the epileptic boy dubious about Jesus' ability to help even while appealing to him (Mark 9:22). Even though Martha confessed Jesus to be the Messiah, the Son of God (John 11:27), she looked for help, not from him directly, but through his prayer to God (John 11:22).[14]

Nevertheless, Jesus encouraged men to look to him directly for help. When the centurion saw in him one "having authority" who need only "say the word" to heal his servant, Jesus commended his faith (Matt. 8:5-13). When a paralytic was brought to him for healing, he saw a deeper need, and forgave his sins, claiming for himself a prerogative which was rightly understood to belong only to God (Matt. 9:2-7). In the storm on Galilee the disciples addressed their plea to him, "Save, Lord, we are perishing." In response, Jesus commanded the storm to cease, and there was calm (Matt. 8:24-27).

In their wonder over his power, the disciples could hardly have failed to note the similarity between this power and that which belongs to God, of whom it is written that the "stormy wind fulfills his command" (Ps. 148:8). In such incidents Jesus was encouraging men to pray to him for such help as could come only from God.

But Jesus not only taught by implication that prayer should be made to him; he stated it explicitly. His words recorded in Matt. 11:28 must so be understood: "Come to me . . . and I will give you rest." In the previous verse he has spoken of the relationship between himself and the Father, so that the distinction (not division) between Father and Son is clearly in view. But he exhorts the weary to come, not to the Father, but to himself (*pros me*). And he emphasizes the fact that <u>he</u> will grant them rest *(kagō anapausō humas)*. But the "coming" clearly implies prayer - the prayer of commitment, the prayer of petition for rest.[15] Jesus here designates himself as the proper Object of prayer.

Another such passage is found in John 14:14: " . . . if you ask me anything in my name, I will do it" (RSV, mg.). The inclusion of *me* is supported by the textual evidence,[16] and is also appropriate because of the emphatic "I" at the end of the verse *(egō poiēso).* Jesus here points to himself as the one to whom prayer is to be addressed, and indicates that he himself will answer prayer.[17]

There is a statement of Jesus in John 16:23 which might seem to deny that prayer is to be addressed to him after his resurrection: "In that day ye shall ask me nothing . . . Whatsoever ye shall ask the Father in my name, he will give it you" (KJV). But the meaning is indicated clearly in Greek: the significant phrases are: *eme ouk erōtēsete ouden . . . an ti aitēsete ton patera . . .* The contrast is not that the disciples will ask the Father instead of the Son, when the Son is no longer with them; rather, the contrast is in the kind of asking. *Erōtaō*, here contrasted with *aiteō*, denotes a request for information. It has just been used in that sense in v.19. Because of the fullness of revelation which will come with the sending of the Spirit, there will no longer need to be this kind of request for instruction.

As a result of such indirect and direct teaching, believers in the New Testament are found, with approval, addressing prayer to Jesus Christ, explicitly ascribing to him what belongs to God alone. Following the resurrection, Thomas addresses him as "My Lord and my God," and Jesus responds by pronouncing a blessing upon those who come to possess similar faith (John 20:28, 29). Peter did not hesitate to ascribe to Jesus omniscience: "Lord, you know everything" (John 21:17). Stephen died commending his spirit, not to the Father, but to Jesus (Acts 7:59). The common expression for prayer, "calling upon the name of the Lord," can be used to speak of prayer addressed to the Son (Acts 9:21).

The teaching of the Scripture on prayer, then, stresses that prayer is to be made to God alone, and yet it also indicates that prayer may be made to more than one person. The contexts of both Matt. 11:28 and John 14:14 reveal that such a distinction exists between Father and Son that one can be known by the other (Matt. 11:27); that the Son can himself pray to the Father (Matt. 11:25; John 14:16); and the Father can command the Son (John 14:31). The Holy Spirit does not appear explicitly in Scripture as the Object of prayer; but in John he appears plainly as a distinct person, who is sent by the Father (John 14:16), and who will bear witness of the Son (John 15:26). When to this is added evidence of the Spirit's deity (as, for example, is found in Acts 5:3, 4), then the data justifies a statement such as that in which Calvin summarized the doctrine of the Trinity: "that Father and Son and Spirit are one God, yet the Son is not the Father, nor the Spirit the Son, but that they are differentiated by a peculiar quality."[18]

So the doctrine of the Trinity does not contradict the Biblical teaching about prayer, but is in fact an integral part of that teaching. Not only with regard to the Object of prayer, but also and especially with regard to the distinctive work of the Son and the Spirit in prayer, there is indeed a difference in function which must be pointed out.

But, as Tillich inquires, how is tritheism then to be avoided? He implies that it cannot.

The answer does not lie in developing a Trinitarian statement in which it becomes logically and rationally clear how one divine essence can subsist wholly in each of three distinct hypostases. Rather what is required is a submission to the self-revelation of the God who cannot be limited by human reason. In such a spirit, Tillich's question, whether prayer to one of the personae is directed toward someone different from another of the three, may be answered in the affirmative, if the word "different" is understood as meaning "capable of being distinguished from another." But if "different" is understood to mean "separate," or "altogether different," then the question must be answered negatively. Probably no better description can be found of the way in which the Trinity is to be perceived than that which Calvin attributes to Gregory of Nazianzus: "I cannot think on the one without quickly being encircled by the splendor of the three; nor can I discern the three without being straightway carried back to the one."[19] A prayer addressed to the Father does not regard him as existing or acting in isolation from the Son and Spirit; only, for the moment, he is in the focus of attention.

That a distinction of persons does not inevitably lead to

tritheism is indicated by the emphasis upon the unity of the persons in the very contexts in which the distinction between them appears. Thus, just before designating himself as the Object and answerer of prayer, Jesus stresses the essential unity between himself and the Father: " . . . no one knows the Son except the Father, and no one knows the Father except the Son . . ." (Matt. 11:27). Again, in the Farewell Discourse: "Believe me that I am in the Father and the Father in me . . ." (John 14:11). It is possible to distinguish between the persons of the Godhead in prayer, but this does not mean that they are regarded as separate entities.

While the doctrine of the Trinity does not present insoluble difficulties for the practice of prayer, it does raise a practical question. In terms of the Biblical teaching, is prayer to be addressed to the triune God, to each of the persons equally, or to one of the persons in distinction from the others? To put the question another way, since a difference of function may be assigned to the three persons, does the role of the Hearer of prayer belong more especially to one of the persons than to the others?

It has already been shown that the Scripture gives examples, and even commands, that prayer is to be addressed to the Son as well as to the Father. This is in harmony with the view that in each of the persons the whole essence of God is to be found. Since prayer to God is always proper, any of the persons may be addressed in prayer. On this basis, prayer addressed to the Holy Spirit is proper, even though Scripture does not speak explicitly of such prayer. Because the essence of God is undivided, it is also proper to address prayer to the triune God, without making a distinction of persons.[20]

But while prayer to any of the persons, or to the three together, is proper, Scripture teaches that prayer is ordinarily to be addressed to the Father. The New Testament pattern for prayer is that it is made to the Father, through the Son, by means of the Holy Spirit.

In order to show that the Father has a distinctive role as the Object of prayer, it is necessary to examine the significance of the use of "Father" as a form of address in New Testament prayer.

The evidence that prayer is characteristically addressed to the Father in the New Testament is conclusive. In the recorded prayers of Jesus, all but one have this form of address.[21] Not only did Jesus himself address the Father in prayer, but he taught the disciples to do so. This is apparent not only in the giving of the

Lord's Prayer (Matt. 6:6-15; Luke 11:2-13), but also in the statements about prayer in the Farewell Discourse (John 15:16; 16:23).[22] On the basis of this example and instruction, the early church was in the habit of praying to the Father.[23] Even the Aramaic word which Jesus had used for Father, "Abba," persisted in the prayers of Greek-speaking Christians (Rom. 8:15; Gal. 4:6).

But what is the meaning of "Father" as used in prayer? Joachim Jeremias has given attention to this question.[24] He holds that there is no precedent for an individual to address God as Father, either in the Old Testament or in Palestinian Judaism prior to the time of Christ. This is not to say that the concept of God as Father was unknown, but that God was not addressed in an intimate way as Father. To do so, Jeremias believes, was an innovation traceable directly to Jesus himself.[25]

Jeremias does not, however, interpret the use of "Father" as an address in prayer in a Trinitarian way. He regards its significance as lying in a new understanding of the nature of God. That Jesus may address God as "my Father" is due to the fullness of the revelation God has granted to him. "Jesus' use of abba expresses his certainty that he is in possession of the revelation because the Father has granted him complete divine knowledge."[26] Jesus need not be more than a man to call God "my Father;" in commending this form of address to his disciples he indicated that they also may participate in the divine sonship.[27] His uniqueness lies only in the completeness of the revelation given to him.[28] In Jeremias' view, then, "Father" does not denote one of the persons of the Godhead, but is a title which denotes the authority and benevolence of God.

It is not to be denied that the name "Father" contains a revelation of God's authority and benevolence. This is certainly the point of Jesus' analogy in Luke 11:11-13, in which a father's love for his children is used as an indication of God's willingness to answer prayer. The authority of God as Father is spoken of in Heb. 12:7: "God is treating you as sons; for what son is there whom his father does not discipline?" It is for this reason that the exposition of the Lord's Prayer has generally taken the address, "Our Father, who art in heaven," as an encouragement to come to God. As Calvin says,

"It is as if we addressed him: 'O Father, who dost abound with great devotion toward thy children, and with great readiness to forgive, we thy children call upon thee . . .

persuaded that thou bearest toward us only the affection of a
father, although we are unworthy of such a father.' "[29]

But beyond this, the use of "Father" in prayer points to a
distinct person of the Godhead. When Jesus prays to his Father in
heaven, there are indications that the relationship in which he stands
to the Father is unique in kind as well as in degree. This is seen in
the fact that (as Jeremias notes),[30] Jesus never joins with his disciples
in saying "our Father," and that a distinction can be seen in his
statements about "my Father" as against what he says about "your
Father." For example, when he speaks about creaturely dependence,
he uses the expression "your Father" (Matt. 6:8, 32); he himself
stands in no such relationship with the Father. Thus, when Jesus
prays to the Father, he is not praying as a creature to his Creator,
nor is he praying to himself. By the term "Father," he designates
the first person of the Trinity.

The use of "Father" in prayer on the part of believers is
different, then, from its use by Christ - but not totally so. For it
denotes the same person in both cases. It is apparent in the prayers
of the early church that to pray to the Father means not only to
pray to the God who acts toward us in a fatherly way, but to pray
to the Father as distinguished from the Son and Spirit. Frequently
the names of the Son and Spirit occur in the same context: " . . . I
bow my knees before the Father . . . that . . . he may grant you to be
strengthened with might through his Spirit in the inner man, and
that Christ may dwell in your hearts through faith . . ." (Eph. 3:14-
17); " . . . do everything in the name of the Lord Jesus, giving
thanks to God the Father through him" (Col. 3:17). Even when the
word "Father" is not used, "God" may refer to him in distinction
from Son and Spirit (cf. Acts 4:24-28). In most cases, prayer in the
early church is prayer to God the Father, the first person of the
Trinity.

Thus it appears that, while prayer to the Son or to the Spirit
is not improper, that the normal pattern is for prayer to be addressed
specifically to the Father as the one who hears and answers prayer.
At the same time, the believer does not divide the work of the
Father from that of the Son and Spirit, but is conscious that his
prayer involves the gracious working of Father, Son and Spirit in
perfect and unbroken unity.

chapter iv

the role of jesus christ in prayer

The Biblical data concerning the place which Jesus Christ has in Christian prayer may be divided into two categories: that which presents him as a teacher of prayer, and that which presents him as the mediator between God and man in prayer. He is a teacher of prayer; not the only one, for others have taught about prayer, and, under the inspiration of the Spirit, have done so infallibly. But he is the mediator; in this he stands alone, performing a function in relation to prayer which no other can perform.

A.   Jesus' Teaching About Prayer

Jesus Christ is not the only teacher of prayer in the Bible. His doctrine stands in continuity with the teaching of the Old Testament; and after him Paul, James, and the writer of Hebrews, among others, add valuable instruction. But among all the teachers of prayer Jesus stands preeminent. The Bible records more teaching about prayer from him than from any other. The church has based its thought about prayer primarily upon the words of Jesus. The Lord's Prayer has not only occupied a place in the worship of the church, but it has in all ages formed the basis for catechetical instruction and theological reflection on prayer.[1] That Jesus regarded his teaching as essential for the proper practice of prayer is indicated by his saying, "If you abide in me and my words abide in you, ask whatever you will, and it shall be done for you" (John 15:7).

The teaching of Jesus about prayer is not limited to his words. It is significant that the request of the disciples for instruction in prayer was made as they observed Jesus at prayer (Luke 11:1). It is taking a very superficial view of Christ to say, as George Buttrick does, that his uniqueness is to be attributed to his communion with God in prayer.[2] But it is true that the prayer life of Jesus, like other aspects of his life, was exemplary, and worthy of our imitation.

Heb. 5:7 speaks of the prayer-experience of Jesus as one of the aspects of his identification with mankind: "In the days of his flesh, Jesus offered up prayers and supplications, with loud cries and tears, to him who was able to save him from death, and he was heard for his godly fear." Calvin regards this passage as giving practical instruction for prayer: " . . . what better guidance can we have as to prayer than the example of Christ? He betook himself immediately to the Father. And thus the Apostle indicates what ought to be done by us when he says that he offered prayers to him who was able to deliver him from death . . ."[3] While only glimpses are given of the prayer life of Christ, yet what is given is full of instruction.[4]

Jesus Christ, then, is the foremost teacher of Christian prayer, whose teaching and example set a pattern for prayer which is valid in all ages.[5]

B.   Jesus' Work as the Mediator for Prayer

Since speech assumes some kind of relationship, prayer occurs within the framework of the relationship between a man (or a community) and God. It would be possible, and proper, to develop the teaching of Scripture on man's estrangement from God, and the means of his reconciliation to God, and then to apply those general teachings to the specific subject of prayer. By such a procedure, it could be shown how the redemptive work of Christ is related to prayer.

However, it is not necessary to follow this indirect method of investigation, since within the Scripture itself the connection between Christ's work and prayer is explicitly stated. A consideration of the passages where this is done will be sufficient to show how prayer depends for its efficacy upon the mediatorial work of Christ.

1.   Prayer in the Name of Christ

The first set of passages, connecting prayer with Christ, is found in John's Gospel. In the Farewell Discourse, the Saviour spoke repeatedly of prayer in his name. He promised that whatever was asked in his name (*en tōi onomati mou*) would be granted (John 14:13, 14; 15:16). Not only that, but the answer would also be given in his name (John 16:23). Finally, he indicated that to ask in his name was something new, a privilege not hitherto enjoyed by the disciples (John 16:24, 26). To these passages may be added Eph. 5:20: " . . . giving thanks in the name of our Lord Jesus Christ to God the Father."

A common view of the meaning of prayer in Christ's name is that adopted by Godet in earlier editions of his commentary on John: "To ask in the name of anyone is, in ordinary life, to ask in place of a person, as if on his part, and applying to oneself, in virtue of his recommendation, all his titles to the favour demanded."[6] With this explanation, prayer in Christ's name would be prayer made on the basis of a right granted by Christ. The believer would have Christ's authorization to apply to the Father for favors due to Christ. While such an interpretation is not out of harmony with Scriptural teaching, it is not satisfactory here because it does not fit those statements in the context which speak of the Father acting in Christ's name (John 14:26; 16:23). It is not inappropriate, due to the economy of redemption, to speak of the Son acting on the authority of the Father (cf. John 8:42), but nowhere does the Scripture speak of the Father acting on the authority of the Son.

Thus a more satisfactory interpretation of the phrase, "in my name," as Godet indicates, places emphasis upon the revelatory character of the name of Jesus Christ: to pray in the name of Christ is " . . . to ask a thing of God as Father on the foundation of the revelation which Jesus has given us of Himself and of His work . . ."[7] The en marks the sphere within which the asking occurs - within the boundaries of the revelation of the person and work of Christ, and taking the fullness of that revelation into account.

With this interpretation, it becomes clear how the activity of the Father can be in the name of the Son. The Father sends the Holy Spirit in the name of Christ (John 14:26), that is, in connection with what is revealed concerning his work of redemption, in harmony with, and in fulfillment of, that work. Likewise, the Father answers prayer, in the name of Christ (John 16:23), not in that the Son authorized him to do so, but rather in connection with the redemptive work of the Son. Answers to prayer are given within the sphere of the revelation embodied in the name of Jesus Christ.

Other statements of Jesus become clear when the name of Christ is understood to refer to the revelation concerning his person and work. It is not strange to speak of prayer being made to Christ in his own name (John 14:14, RSV mg.), when that is understood to mean "in harmony with what is included in his name." And it becomes plain in what sense prayer in Christ's name is a new privilege (John 16:24). Certainly, as Calvin notes, even in the Old Testament "It was . . . one of the principles of faith, that prayers offered to God when there was no Mediator were rash and useless." Yet, believers then " . . . did not clearly and fully understand what was meant."[8] That is, the name of Christ was not yet fully known.

When the revelation was complete - the "day" to which Jesus refers (John 16:23, 26) is the time of his resurrection, which would usher in a new era of spiritual privileges - then prayer would stand on a new level. "From the time that Christ gave His life for His friends . . . and for their salvation sat down at the right hand of God . . . His name would become to them, in quite a new sense, the pledge and guarantee of their prayer being heard."[9]

Jesus' statements that prayer must be "in his name" cannot be fully understood when taken by themselves; they presuppose a knowledge of the revelation which is embodied in the name of our Lord Jesus Christ. Calvin's comment on this phrase, that "We are said to pray in the name of Christ when we take him as our Advocate, to reconcile us, and make us find favour with his Father . . .,"[10] represents his judgment as to the central meaning of the name of Christ. As subsequent study will show, his interpretation is valid. But beyond that aspect of the revelation contained in Christ's name, there is also to be found the encouragement of the manifestation which Christ gave of the power and grace of God, and the guidance as to prayer's content which comes from a knowledge of God's will.[11] Prayer in Christ's name involves not only dependence on his mediation, but participation in the life which comes from him and submission to his teaching.

2.   Christ as the High Priest of Prayer

It is in his priestly office that Christ performs his distinctive work in relation to prayer, and this work is most clearly described in the Epistle to the Hebrews.

The priestly work of Christ is first connected with prayer in Heb. 4:14-16: "Since then we have a great high priest who has passed through the heavens, Jesus, the Son of God, let us hold fast our confession . . . Let us then with confidence draw near to the throne of grace, that we may receive mercy and find grace to help. in time of need."

Although none of the usual words for prayer appears in this passage, it unmistakably deals with prayer. The Oriental imagery of approaching the throne calls to mind Esther's entrance into the presence of King Ahasuerus to present a request (Esther 5:1-4). Here the one who occupies the throne is not identified; but when the statement that Jesus as our great high priest has passed through the heavens is taken with the later assertion that "Christ has entered . . . into heaven itself, now to appear in the presence of God on our behalf (Heb. 9:24), it is plain that a heavenly throne is in view, and that the King who occupies it is God himself.[12] It also is clear that the purpose of approaching God is to receive help. The drawing near is not a once-for-all act, nor an entrance into God's presence at death; for *proserchōmetha* is a present subjunctive, and the grace that is sought is *eis eukairon boētheian* - "for timely assistance" in the face of trials. What is in view, then, is coming to God in prayer for strength to face the temptations of daily life, the constant pressure to abandon one's profession of faith in Christ.

This approach to God in prayer is to be "with boldness" (Heb. 4:16).[13] The term *parrēsia* has the basic meaning of openness, and when used of a person's attitude toward God denotes his lack of shame and fear.[14] Of course there can be a false confidence, a boldness that amounts to brashness in approaching God. But the writer of Hebrews here speaks of a confidence before God which is justified; its basis has been stated in the preceding verses.[15]

Confidence in approaching God is justified because of the fact that believers possess a great high priest in Jesus, the Son of God (Heb. 4:14). Since Heb. 4:14-16 is an introductory passage, which begins the detailed discussion of Christ's priesthood, it is not stated in these verses what that priesthood signifies. However, the manner in which the priesthood is exercised is stated. Christ, as our priest, is able to sympathize with weak and tempted men, since he also was tempted (Heb. 4:15). This sympathy extends to the experience of prayer, for Jesus also prayed in the face of temptation (Heb. 5:7). Therefore prayer is made with the confidence that in the presence of the Father there is one who is able to enter fully into the needs which are being expressed. What a powerful encouragement this is to believers has been finely stated by John Murray:

> "And the thought that we in the stresses and conflicts associated with the body of our humiliation are objects of the solicitude and compassion of him who sits at the right hand of the throne of the majesty in the heavens and who dispenses from the reservoir of his knowledge and experience consolation, fellow-feeling, and strength injects into our fainting hearts the confidence of his invincible grace."[16]

The explication of what is involved in the priesthood of Christ occupies much of the Epistle to the Hebrews;[17] the essential points of it are brought out in a passage at the close of the discussion:

"Therefore, brethren, since we have confidence to enter the sanctuary by the blood of Jesus, by the new and living way which he opened for us through the curtain, that is, through his flesh, and since we have a great high priest over the house of God, let us draw near with a true heart in full assurance of faith, with our hearts sprinkled clean from an evil conscience and our bodies washed with pure water. Let us hold fast the confession of our hope without wavering" (Heb. 10:19-23).

It will be noted that there is a very close parallelism between Heb. 4:14-16 and Heb. 10:19-23. Both passages contain exhortations to maintain the confession of faith and to draw near to God, on the basis of the possession of Christ as high priest. Both use the term *parrēsia* to describe the manner in which a believer may approach God. Because of this parallelism, the *proserchōmetha* of Heb. 10:22 is to be understood as a reference to prayer, even though in this passage the petitionary aspect of the "drawing near" is not stated.

In Heb. 10:19, the place to which approach is made is "the sanctuary" *(tōn hagiōn, genitive plural of to hagion).*[18] In the ninth chapter of Hebrews, it is plain that "the sanctuary" is the antitype of the Holy of Holies of the Mosaic tabernacle. Just as the high priest entered the innermost part of the tabernacle once a year (Heb. 9:7), so Christ as the antitypal high priest has entered the heavenly sanctuary once for all: "For Christ has entered, not into a sanctuary made with hands, a copy of the true one, but into heaven itself, now to appear in the presence of God on our behalf" (Heb. 9:24). The sanctuary is thus identified as the presence of God. Heb. 10:19 speaks of access to the presence of God, the privilege which believers have of approaching God in prayer. This is equivalent to approaching the throne of grace as is shown by the statement that Christ our high priest is " . . . seated at the right hand of the throne of the Majesty in heaven . . .," where he acts as a minister of the sanctuary (Heb. 8:1, 2).

The exhortation to prayer rests upon the possession of believers of "confidence to enter the sanctuary by the blood of Jesus" (Heb. 10:19). The phrase *en toi haimati Iēsou* indicates the means by which entrance into God's presence is possible. This statement refers back to Heb. 9:12, in which it is said that Christ's entrance into the sanctuary was through his blood. But why should it be that Christ, the Son of God, who was without sin (Heb. 4:15), was barred from the presence of God, so that only through his blood could he find admittance? The answer lies in the nature of the priestly office of Christ, which is unfolded in this epistle.

As high priest, Jesus Christ identified himself with his people (Heb. 2:9-18). Because of this solidarity with sinful men, Christ could not appear in the presence of God as their representative unless he dealt with their sin. But sins cannot be forgiven apart from the shedding of blood (Heb. 9:22), and the blood of animal sacrifices only served for ceremonial cleansing, not for cleansing of the conscience before God (Heb. 9:13; 10:4). Hence, the blood of Jesus signifies the offering of the antitypal sacrifice, a sacrifice which effectively removes the guilt of sin: " . . . he has appeared once for all at the end of the age to put away sin by the sacrifice of himself" (Heb. 9:26). It is because he has thus offered his life as a satisfaction for the sins of his people that he is able to appear in the presence of God in their behalf (Heb. 9:24).

But it is not only the case that Jesus Christ stands in God's presence representing his people. He is the forerunner (*prodromos*), in whose steps believers are to follow (Heb. 6:20; cf. 12:1, 2). For the entrance made possible by his sacrifice is a way for us (Heb. 10:20), a way which believers are to travel. By virtue of their solidarity with the great high priest, and on the basis of the satisfaction for their sins which he has made, believers are able to follow him into the presence of God, as they pray. As Delitzsch has said, "Christ, in high-priestly wise, has preceded us . . . we follow Him along the way which He has opened and formed for us, knowing ourselves to be now reconciled and sanctified by the one oblation (*prosphora*) of His blood outpoured on earth and presented in heaven."[19]

The further description which is given of the way of access to God, in Heb. 10:20, has given rise to an amazing variety of interpretations. Without entering into all the questions which arise, the significance of this description of the *hodos* for prayer may be briefly indicated.

The way is described as *prosphaton*. This term means literally "recently killed," but in its later usage had the more general meaning of "new" or "fresh" (cf. Acts 18:2; Eccl. 1:9 LXX). Many have taken this to mean that access to the presence of God was unavailable before Christ came.[20] However, it is clear that believers in the Old Testament enjoyed fellowship with God, were conscious that their sins were forgiven, and that their prayers were answered. This is not because they had another way of coming to God than through the one great sacrifice of Christ. Rather, the death of Christ, as foreordained by God and therefore certain, was effective for the forgiveness of the sins of the elect even before it actually occurred in history. The blood which Christ shed was "The blood of the eternal covenant" (Heb. 13:20), efficacious in all ages (cf. Rev. 13:8). Hence the way to God must be understood to be "new", not in the sense that it was opened for the first time at the death of Christ, but in that it was now more clearly seen and understood by believers. This view is supported by the statement that " . . . the way into the sanctuary had not yet been manifested (*pephanerōsthai*) while the first tabernacle had standing" (Heb. 9:8 - trans. by W.S.). The way then, is not absolutely new, but only relatively so, in terms of the fuller understanding and assurance possessed by believers under the new Covenant.[21] At the same time, it must be stressed that this newness is not only subjective; it is based upon the objective fullness of revelation which accompanied the actual accomplishment in history of Christ's redemptive work.

The way of access is further described as *zōsan* - "living" (Heb. 10:20). This cannot mean "effective" in contrast to the deadness of the Old Testament system, for by means of the types and shadows, Old Testament saints experienced genuine communion with God. "Living" might indicate that the Mosaic system, as fulfilled and abrogated, is now dead, and that Christians therefore should resist the temptation to turn back to it. But it seems likely that, beyond this, the "living way" points to the fact that access to God involves a vital personal union with Christ. Coming to God involves more than an intellectual understanding that propitiation for sin has been made; it requires entering into a relationship with the high priest who is a living person.

The expression "through the curtain, that is, through his flesh" (Heb. 10:20) is especially difficult. It may be that the bodily suffering of Christ was offensive to the Hebrew Christians to whom this letter was written, so that it was necessary to stress that entrance into God's presence was only by means of (*dia* with genitive) that suffering. Calvin has probably captured the sense of the symbolism here when he says that the flesh of Christ " . . . conceals as a veil the majesty of God, while it is also that which conducts us to the enjoyment of all the good things of God."[22] Both the objective right to enter God's presence, and the subjective assurance of that right, depend upon the fact that " . . . the Word became flesh, and dwelt among us . . ." (John 1:14), and that he was " . . . put to death in the flesh . . ." (I Pet. 3:18).

One other reason is given as a basis of the exhortation to prayer: " . . . since we have a great high priest over the house of God" (Heb. 10:21). This is not to say that the priestly work of Christ is something different from the offering of sacrifice which has just been discussed; but that the priestly work of Christ continues. The verb for this sentence is the present participle *echontes*, supplied from v.19. The offering of sacrifice was once for all, not to be repeated (Heb. 9:25, 26). But Christ continues to act as high priest over the house of God. From what has been said earlier in Hebrews it is apparent that this continuing priestly activity involves (1) the exhibition of his blood as the basis on which believers are accepted and blessed by God (Heb. 9:12); (2) intercession for his own (Heb. 7:25); and (3) the actual granting of aid to those who are in need (Heb. 2:18).

The foregoing discussion has presented the way in which prayer depends upon the blood, that is, the sacrifice of Christ. Calvin regards this continuing efficacy of Christ's sacrifice as the essence of his intercession: "But the value of his sacrifice, by which he once pacified God toward us, is always powerful and efficacious; the blood by which he atoned for our sins, the obedience which he rendered, is a continual intercession for us."[23] Such a view, however, runs the risk of suggesting that Christ's intercession concerns only the removal of guilt. But the continuing intercession of Christ is said in Heb. 7:25 to make possible salvation *eis to pantelas* - "to the full extent, salvation complete and perfect."[24] In Rom. 8:34, the intercession of Christ is said to be the basis of assurance that all the assaults of adversaries will not be able to rob believers of eternal enjoyment of the love of God. When to these statements is added an awareness of the long tradition of intercessors who stood before God and presented the needs of their people[25], and the fact that Jesus during his earthly ministry prayed for specific blessings for those who believed in him, (Luke 23:34; John 17) it is apparent that the continuing priestly work of Christ involves petition for his people. As John Murray has said, " . . . the intercession covers the range of what is requisite to and of what is realized in the eschatological salvation."[26]

Is there a relation, then, between the fact that Christ prays for his people and their own prayer? Heb. 10:21, 22 indicates that there is a relation: because Christ exercises a continuing priesthood (which includes the function of intercession) believers are to draw near to God. But it is not stated explicitly how believer's prayers are helped by Christ's intercession. Since the desire to pray and the knowledge of what to pray for are gifts of God, it may be presumed that these are given in answer to Christ's prayer to the Father.[27] Beyond that, the Christian can enjoy confidence as he prays from the consideration that, insofar as he prays according to God's will, his prayer joins that of his great high priest, whose intercession is always availing.

The third aspect of Christ's continuing priesthood, that of granting aid, serves as an encouragement to prayer in that Christ, as a sympathetic high priest, is united with the Father in his throne, and, with the Father, sends the Spirit and answers prayer (John 16:7; 14:14). In this Christ serves as the royal priest " . . . after the order of Melchizedek" (Heb. 5:10).

One other passage needs to be mentioned, in which prayer is related to the work of Christ: I John 1:9 with 2:1, 2. There, the efficacy of prayer for forgiveness (I John 1:9) plainly rests upon the fact that Jesus Christ serves as *parakletos* before the Father (I John 2:1). The aid which he is able to give as "one called alongside to help" consists in the fact that he is *hilasmos . . . peri tōn hamartiōn hēmōn*. The word *hilasmos* means "propitiation," "that which renders (God) favorable."[28] John does not specify how Jesus accomplishes this, but from the usage of the term in the LXX for the sin-offering, and from the discussion of Christ's work in Hebrews, there is no question that the idea of sacrifice is implied. Hence, prayer for forgiveness is said here to depend for its answer upon the priestly work of Christ.

Prayer occupies a prominent place in the teaching of Jesus, and because of both the amount and the profundity of that teaching, he is the teacher par excellence of Christian prayer. But his teaching cannot be isolated from his person and work. By means of his suffering and death he has removed the barrier of sin, so that those who believe in him are reconciled to God. Prayer is one of the privileges of the new relationship between God and the redeemed. Prayer depends not only upon the completed atonement of Christ, but upon his continuing priesthood, in which he pleads the efficacy of his sacrifice, makes intercession for his own, and powerfully succours them. Prayer made in his name takes into account all his teaching, keeping within its bounds, and trusts for its efficacy upon his work in all its aspects. Only such prayer can be confident of acceptance with God. Prayer in all ages has been dependent upon the mediation of Christ; in the Old Testament, believers anticipated the coming of the Messiah, and believed in him through types and prophecies; in the New Testament era, they rest upon his accomplished work and the clearer light of revelation about him. True prayer can be made only by the one who listens to his words: "I am the way, the turth, and the life; no one comes to the Father, but by me" (John 14:6).

chapter v

the work of the holy spirit in prayer

The possibility of prayer rests not only upon the distinctive work of Christ, through which we have access to God, but also upon the work of the Holy Spirit. The Apostle Paul, having asserted that Gentiles who were separated from God " . . . have been brought near in the blood of Christ" (Eph. 2:13), adds that " . . . through him we both have access in one Spirit to the Father" (Eph. 2:18). Christians are to be filled with the Spirit, which condition will be manifested in praise and giving of thanks (Eph. 5:18-20). They are to "Pray at all times in the Spirit, with all prayer and supplication" (Eph. 6:18). Obviously, prayer cannot be fully understood apart from a consideration of the Holy Spirit's work in it.

There are two aspects of the Spirit's work in prayer as revealed in the Scripture: he provides motivation and guidance for prayer in the believer; and he acts as intercessor for the believer.

A.   The Motivation and Guidance for Prayer

In two closely related passages, Paul shows how prayer is the result of the Holy Spirit's presence in the life of the believer. The first passage is Rom. 8:15: "For ye have not received the spirit of bondage again to fear; but ye have received the Spirit of adoption, whereby we cry, Abba, Father" (KJV). The parallel passage is Gal. 4:6: "And because you are sons, God has sent the Spirit of his Son into our hearts, crying, "Abba! Father!" The two passages help to explain one another and should be studied together.

The first fact to be noted is that the *pneuma* of these verses is the Holy Spirit. Both the ARV and RSV have "spirit" (with a small 's') for *pneuma* in both places where the word occurs in Rom. 8:15, while both have Spirit (capital 'S') in Gal. 4:6. But the obvious similarity of the two verses, and the fact that it is plainly the Holy Spirit who is referred to in Rom. 8:14, 16, indicates that Rom. 8:15 refers to the Holy Spirit as well.[1] The Holy Spirit has been sent by the Father (Gal. 4:6; cf. John 14:26), and believers have received him. (Rom. 8:15).

As a result of the Spirit's presence in the believer, there arises from him the cry, "Abba." In Gal. 4:6 it is the Spirit who cries; in Rom. 8:15, believers cry. The connection between those two statements is indicated by the *en hōi* of Rom. 8:15. Since the "Spirit of sonship" means the Holy Spirit, then *en hōi* should be understood as instrumental, meaning "by whom." When Chrisitans cry "Abba," it is the result of the working of the Spirit in them. The cry can be attributed both to the Spirit, and to believers, without any contradiction. The relationship between God and the believer is not merely complementary, as though they stood side by side; but all of the believer's work is at the same time God's work (cf. Phil. 2:12, 13). So, our crying is at the same time the Spirit's crying within us.

The cry of "Abba," in both passages, signifies the status of sonship which is enjoyed by believers since the coming of Christ, in contrast to the servile status that was characteristic of the former dispensation (Gal. 4:7). The Holy Spirit does not initiate this new relationship; he is given to those who are already sons (Gal. 4:6). But the title of "Spirit of adoption" is given him " . . . because it is he who creates in the children of God the filial love and confidence by which they are able to cry 'Abba, Father' and enjoy the rights and privileges of God's children."[2] But it should be noted that the consciousness of the filial relationship comes to expression in prayer. The expression "Abba" is an especially meaningful one. It is an Aramaic word, and thus it is strange that Paul should use it in writing to Greek-speaking people in Rome and Galatia. The reason seems to be that this was the word used by Jesus to address God in prayer, as Mark specifically says (Mark 14:36).[3] "Abba" would have been the word used by Jesus when he gave the Lord's Prayer to the disciples. Thus Paul could appeal to the utterance of this foreign word in writing these epistles, because the people were familiar with its use in prayer. It was not simply their consciousness that God was their Father, but their ability to pray to him as Father, which Paul here attributes to the working of the Holy Spirit. The verb *krazō*, used in both passages, supports this conclusion. The verb denotes loud crying of any kind, but is commonly used in the LXX, especially in the Psalms, of prayer to God.[4] The prayer of Jesus is described by the related term *kraugē* (Heb. 5:7). The loudness of the cry of "Abba" may well express the confidence with which it is uttered: "In calling is expressed the certainty and joy with which

one who is moved by the Spirit turns to God. The address of servants, on the other hand, is the murmured prayer prescribed by
Jewish custom."[5]

The teaching of Rom. 8:15 and Gal. 4:6, then, is that the
believer's ability to pray comes from the Holy Spirit who dwells
within him. It is the Holy Spirit who makes the believer aware of his
status as a child of God, and who opens his eyes to the inheritance
to which he now has a claim (Rom. 8:16, 17). The cry of "Abba"
must include praise and adoration and thanksgiving to the One who
has taken such a guilty and undeserving creature to be his child. It
includes the submission which is appropriate on the part of a son
toward his Father. And it surely involves an application to the
Father for the granting of those benefits which are now the
believer's, and of which he stands in need, including the benefit of
forgiveness. And because he is not the only son, but part of the
household of faith (it is "we" who cry), he does not seek the Father's
blessings for himself alone, but for others as well. Thus, the cry,
"Abba, Father," really implies every aspect of prayer.

We are not dependent upon Rom. 8:15 and Gal. 4:6 alone
for the knowledge that all true prayer is a result of the working of
the Spirit. In order to pray aright, a man must be aware of his real
needs, and he must know that the resources to meet those needs
are to be found in God. But it is the Holy Spirit who convinces men
of sin (John 16:8), and he enables men to see the grace of God
which is available to them (I Cor. 2:9-12). Sinful men neither
honor God nor give thanks to him (Rom. 1:21); hence, prayers of
praise and thanksgiving are impossible unless the Spirit is at work
(Eph. 5:18-20). Prayer for others requires love for them; but love is
the fruit of the Spirit (Gal. 5:22). In short, there is no element of
proper prayer which cannot be traced back to the operation of the
Holy Spirit in the believer's life.

B.   The Spirit's Intercession

Special attention must be given to a passage which speaks
most directly of the Spirit's work in prayer:

> "Likewise the Spirit helps us in our weakness; for we do
> not know how to pray as we ought, but the Spirit himself
> intercedes for us with sighs too deep for words. And he who
> searches the hearts of men knows what is the mind of the
> Spirit, because the Spirit intercedes for the saints according
> to the will of God" (Rom. 8:26, 27).

It is clear that this passage refers to assistance given by the Holy Spirit because of the fact that believers do not know for what to pray.[6] As a remedy for this weakness, the Spirit's work of intercession is set forth.

There have been two main views among Reformed scholars regarding this intercession of the Spirit. Some have held, with Calvin, that it refers to the teaching ministry of the Spirit, who remedies our ignorance of what to pray for by instructing us. As Calvin expresses it, " . . . we are taught by the same Spirit how to pray, and what to ask in our prayers."[7] Abraham Kuyper, on the other hand, views the intercession of the Spirit as an activity wholly distinct from the believer's efforts in prayer: "But being unable of ourselves to kindle the incense, the Holy Spirit helps our infirmities, and from our hearts prays to God in our behalf. We are not conscious of it; He prays for and in us with groans that cannot be uttered; which does not mean that He makes us utter groans for which we cannot account, but that He groans in us . . ."[8] The question, then, is whether Rom. 8:26, 27 refers to the Spirit's enabling believers to pray, or to his prayer for them.

In support of the view that a work of the Spirit distinct from the believer's own praying is meant, the following points must be considered: (1) The verb *sunantilambanetai* (Rom. 8:26) suggests a work of the Spirit that is over against (*anti*) our own, as well as with (*sun*) ours. The kind of action denoted by this verb, according to A. T. Robertson, is " . . . as if two men were carrying a log, one at each end."[9] (2) The phrase *auto to pneuma* (Rom. 8:26) places emphasis upon the fact that the Spirit is the subject of the action: "the Spirit himself." A distinction from the human spirit seems to be implied (cf. Rom. 8:16). (3) The verb *entugchanō* properly means "to appeal" or "petition," and the preposition *huper* adds the idea of "for the benefit of" another (Rom. 8:26, 27). Hence, the Spirit's action here is rightly said to be intercession. The general idea of "helping," i.e. by instructing the believer in what to pray for, does not fit the words that are used.[10] (4) The Spirit's intercession is said to take place in *stenagmois alalētois* - "unuttered or unutterable groanings" (Rom. 8:26). The "groanings," as in Rom. 8:23, indicate deep desire and longing. These desires do not come to articulate expression. In itself, this phrase is not of decisive importance in determining the nature of the Spirit's intercession. It could mean only that the intercession is accompanied with "sighs too deep for words." But taken with the other evidence, it seems to indicate that the Spirit's intercession does not issue in vocal prayer.[11] Therefore the phrase favors the view that the work of the Spirit described here is not instruction regarding the content of prayer; for that would naturally lead to expression of that content once it was grasped by the mind.

These facts justify the conclusion that Rom. 8:26, 27 is describing a work of the Holy Spirit in believers, in which, apart from their conscious volition or understanding, he petitions the Father for those benefits which they need. The assurance is given that this intercession is effective. When it is said in Rom. 8:27 that "he who searches the hearts of men knows what is the mind of the spirit," that would be saying very little if "knows" meant only "to be aware of." When the reason is assigned, "because the Spirit intercedes for the saints according to the will of God," then it is evident that "know" means here "recognizes and approves."[12] The Father grants that for which the Spirit intercedes because it is *kata theon*, that is, in accordance with his nature and purpose.

The information given here is not adequate to determine whether or not the intercession of the Spirit enters into the consciousness of the believer. It is certain that the intercession takes place in the hearts of believers, for it is as the "searcher of hearts" that the Father takes notice of it (Rom. 8:27). Kuyper holds that the believer is entirely unconscious of the Spirit's pleading.[13] Yet, the Spirit is surely not to be located spatially within believers. He is said to dwell in their hearts only in the sense that he is at work there. Hence, it seems that in some sense the groaning must be attributed to the believers as well as to the Spirit. It does not arise from their own understanding and will, but it is from their hearts; it cannot be separated from the new life given them by the indwelling Spirit. John Murray's summary captures the thought of this passage well:

> "As God searches the heart of the children of God he finds unuttered and unutterable groanings. Though they are thus inarticulate, there is a meaning and intent that cannot escape the omniscient eye of God - they are wholly intelligible to him. And, furthermore, they are found to be in accordance with his will . . . because, though surpassing our understanding and utterance, they are indited by the Holy Spirit and are the ways in which his intercessions come to expression in our

consciousness."14

Though Rom. 8:26, 27 does not teach that the Holy Spirit instructs our minds in proper prayer, what was said in connection with the study of Rom. 8:15 and Gal. 4:6 stands - the Christian does possess the ability to pray, and that ability is given him by the Holy Spirit. The Spirit's work of instruction in prayer and his intercession go together. While Abraham Kuyper goes too far in insisting that the Spirit's intercession takes place wholly apart from the believer's consciousness, he has a helpful statement of the relation between these two works of the Spirit in relation to prayer:

> "Apart from the intercession of the Holy Spirit in our behalf there is also a work of His Person in our own prayers . . . The Holy Spirit prays in us as long and in as much as we can not pray for ourselves; but at the same time he teaches us to pray, that gradually His prayer may become superfluous . . ."15

The work of the Holy Spirit is the prerequisite for every aspect of prayer in the believer. Therefore, it is really a continuation of the discussion of his work in prayer as we turn now to consider prayer in its subjective aspects. To be studied are the qualifications which are produced in the saints by the Spirit which enable them to pray; and then the content of prayer as delineated by the same Spirit.

chapter VI

qualifications in the one who prays

Prayer, according to the Bible, involves a personal relationship between God and man. In prayer, man is not manipulating or invoking some unknown Power, but is calling upon the living God. True prayer regards God as a person, who hears and reacts to prayer. Furthermore, the one who prays is not an automaton, but a person who is involved in intercourse with God. Therefore, the form and words of a prayer are important only as they are the genuine expression of the thoughts and desires of a person. That this is the case appears from the emphasis in the Bible upon the personal state of the one who would pray aright. According to Scripture, the person who prays must be reverent, submissive, sincere, believing, and obedient.

A.   Reverence

The Old Testament emphasizes the need for reverence in approaching God. The regulations of the ceremonial law, the striking acts of judgment when men dealt carelessly with holy things (Lev. 10:1-3; I Chron. 13:5-10, etc.), served to impress upon God's people his holiness and transcendence. There is warning about irreverence in prayer:

"Guard your steps when you go to the house of God; to draw near to listen is better than to offer the sacrifice of fools . . . Be not rash with your mouth, nor let your heart be hasty to utter a word before God, for God is in heaven, and you upon earth; therefore let your words be few" (Eccl. 5:1, 2).

When Jesus taught his disciple to use a child's word for Father, "Abba," in speaking to God, he was not repudiating the need for reverence in prayer. In the Lord's Prayer, there is a qualification; God is to be addressed as "Our Father who art in heaven . . ." (Matt. 6:9). As Calvin indicates, these words are not meant to "locate" God, as though he were in heaven and therefore not on earth. But, " . . . it is as if he had been said to be of infinite greatness or loftiness, or incomprehensible essence, of boundless might, and of everlasting immortality."[1] Even in approaching God as Father, men are to be aware of the distance which separates his divinity from their humanity. And so the petition follows, "Hallowed be thy name" (Matt. 6:9). That is (as the Heidelberg Catechism has it), " . . . help us first of all to know thee rightly, and to hallow, glorify and praise thee in all thy works through which there shine thine almighty power, wisdom, goodness, righteousness, mercy, and truth."[2] Reflection on the majesty, power, and purity of God leads to a reverent attitude in prayer.

B.   Sincerity

Jesus' rebuke of the Jewish religious leaders included a denunciation of their hypocrisy in prayer. "And when you pray, you must not be like the hypocrites; for they love to stand and pray in the synagogues and at the street corners, that they may be seen by men" (Matt. 6:5). "Beware of the scribes, who . . . for a pretence make long prayers" (Mark 12:40). Behind such hypocrisy lay the self-satisfaction of such leaders. Their prayers were unreal because they had no sense of their own need, and therefore no real desire for the grace of God.

The Scriptures not only condemn hypocritical prayer, but speak positively of the need for sincerity in prayer. Jesus warned against the heaping up of empty phrases in prayer (Matt. 6:7, 8); yet in two of his parables he encouraged persistence in prayer when an answer is delayed (Luke 11:5-8; 18:1-7). He certainly did not mean that by mere mechanical repetition God's resistance is broken down. The force of these parables is obviously in an implied contrast between the sleepy friend and the unjust judge on the one hand, and God on the other. Importunate prayer reflects faith which is not vanquished by lack of immediate results (cf. Matt. 15:22-28); but it also implies fervent desire, an unwillingness to be content unless the request is granted. Descriptions of exemplary instances of prayer often include the fact that such prayers were made with earnestness. The publican who prayed for mercy "beat his breast" as an indication of the strength of his emotion (Luke 11:13). Christ's prayers were made with "loud cries and tears" (Heb. 5:7); in Gethsemane he prayed "more earnestly" (Luke 22:44). When Peter was imprisoned, "earnest" prayer was made for him by the church (Acts 12:5). Elijah is said to have prayed "fervently" (James 5:17).[3]

Calvin makes it one of the basic rules of prayer, " . . . that in our petitions we ever sense our own insufficiency, and earnestly pondering how we need all that we seek, join with this prayer an earnest - nay, burning-desire to attain it . . . Now what do we account more hateful . . . to God than the fiction of someone asking pardon for his sins, all the while either thinking he is not a sinner, or at least not thinking he is a sinner?"[4]

C.   Submission

Feverent desire, of course, does not stand by itself as a requirement for prayer. For the sovereignty of God demands that human desire be submissive to his will.

The foremost example of submissive prayer is that of Jesus in Gethsemane: "My Father, if it be possible, let this cup pass from me; nevertheless, not as I will, but as thou wilt" (Matt. 26:39). The believer, if he prays sincerely, manifests a similar attitude when he prays, "Thy will be done on earth as it is in heaven" (Matt. 6:10). In asking this, Calvin says, " . . . we renounce the desires of our flesh; for whoever does not resign and submit his feelings to God opposes as much as he can God's will, since only what is corrupt comes forth from us."[5]

Paul's experience in prayer indicates how submission places bounds upon importunity in prayer. He prayed three times for the removal of his thorn; but when it was revealed to him that it was not God's will to remove it, he gladly submitted to the will of the Father (II Cor. 12:8, 9).

This attitude of submission in prayer does not remain merely a kind of restraint, in that one does not insist on his own will as ultimate. But, in so far as the will of God is revealed, and hence is known, submission involves embracing that will, and desiring that it be done. Submission to God's will determines in a positive way the content of prayer. Prayer made in submission to God thus comes to be prayer "according to his will" (I John 5:14).[6]

D.   Faith

Scripture clearly indicates that faith is an essential condition for efficacious prayer. Jesus stated this positively when he said, "And whatever you ask in prayer, you will receive, if you have faith" (Matt. 21:21). The condition is stated negatively by James, when he says concerning the man praying for wisdom, "But let him ask in faith, nothing doubting; for he that doubteth is like the surge of the sea driven by the wind and tossed. For let not that man think that he shall receive anything of the Lord . . ." (James 1:6, 7 ARV).[7]

The content of faith is not stated in these two passages. But their contexts, and other passages in which faith in relation to prayer is discussed, show that this faith does have a definite content. "The prayer of faith" (James 5:15) is prayer which involves the conviction that certain things are true, that a certain state of affairs actually exists.

Much of the preceding discussion has dealt with the objective facts which make prayer possible. It has been necessary, all along, to speak of the faith-content which is implicit in true prayer. What remains to be done here is to show that when faith is mentioned in Scripture as a condition of prayer, it means a believing of these facts as true. It will be seen that faith involves an inward conviction of the truth of God's existence, power, and benevolence; and, in connection with the latter, of the efficacy of Christ's redemptive work.

1.   Belief in the Existence of God

That prayer involves belief in the existence of a Hearer of prayer might seem so obvious as not to require statement. However, the existence of an altar to an unknown god, to which Paul refers (Acts 17:23), points to the possibility of prayer as a "shot in the dark," made on the chance that such a prayer might be heard and answered. And there are contemporary attempts to maintain prayer in the absence of belief in a personal God capable of hearing prayer.[8] Hence it is not without reason that the writer of Hebrews says that " . . . without faith it is impossible to please him. For whoever would draw near to God must believe that he exists . . ." (Heb. 11:6). Paul indicates that the faith which is essential for prayer is belief in God when he asks, "But how are men to call upon him in whom they have not believed? And how are they to believe in him of whom they have not heard?" (Rom. 10:14). Faith here is clearly understood to be a believing acceptance of the revelation about God which has been given to men.

2.   Belief in the Power of God

A number of passages emphasize the fact that faith involves awareness of, and confidence in, God's unlimited power. In Hebrews, the God whose existence is believed is the God who created the world by his word of power (Heb. 11:3).

On a number of occasions Jesus taught that faith is a belief in God's omnipotence. He noted the greatness of the faith of the centurion, who was confident that simply by speaking a word of command, Jesus was able to heal his servant (Matt. 8:8-10). He asked the blind men who sought healing, "Do you believe that I am able to do this?" Upon their affirmative reply, he said, "According to your faith be it done to you" (Matt. 9:27-29). The father of the epileptic boy was unsure whether Jesus was able to help or not; Jesus indicated that he lacked faith (Mark 9:17-24).

In these incidents, faith is seen to be confidence that nothing is beyond the power of the one in whom it is placed. The faith necessary for prayer is the kind of faith exemplified by Abraham: "No distrust made him waver concerning the promise of God, but he grew strong in his faith as he gave glory to God, fully convinced that God was able to do what he had promised" (Rom. 4:20, 21).

3.   Belief in God's Benevolence

A number of passages point to God's willingness to grant help as the content of faith. Heb. 11:6 says that beyond faith in God's existence, there is necessary for prayer the persuasion that he is the "rewarder" of those who seek him. In James 1:5, 6 the statement that prayer must be made in faith is preceded by the assertion that God " . . . gives to all men generously and without reproaching . . ." Jesus declared that the faith of the Canaanite woman was great (Matt. 15:22-28). Her faith was manifested in the fact that she continued to ask for mercy in the face of an apparent rebuff; her importunity rested upon an unshakeable conviction of the Saviour's mercy.

Faith in God's benevolence does not exist in isolation from an awareness of his holiness, and of one's own sinfulness. Faith also takes into account the fact that " . . . the wrath of God is revealed from heaven against all ungodliness and wickedness of men . . ." (Rom. 1:18). Therefore, genuine faith in God's benevolence is necessarily faith in Jesus Christ, who has removed the barrier of sin between God and the redeemed by his obedience and sacrifice. The faith which is essential for prayer is faith in his finished work; in him " . . . we have boldness and confidence of access through our faith in him" (Eph. 3:12). The believer depends for God's acceptance of his prayer upon all that has been revealed concerning the high priestly work of Christ.

When faith refers to a belief in the revelation concerning the nature of God and the work of Jesus Christ, it is easy to see why doubt makes prayer to be ineffective. To doubt God's existence, or power, or benevolence, is to deny God himself. It is an insult to his Name to regard anything as too hard for him (cf. Jer. 32:17, 27). To think of him as unwilling to help is to imply that evil men, who respond to the pleas of their children, are better than God (Matt. 7:9-11). The Epistle to the Hebrews, which develops so fully the doctrine of the priesthood of Christ as the basis for confidence in approaching God, also has very solemn warnings about the sin of unbelief, of "spurning" the Son of God (cf. Heb. 10:23, 26-31).

Doubt with regard to the nature of God as the Hearer of prayer, and the redemption accomplished by Christ, is not weakness of faith, but the lack of it, and is culpable in the sight of God. Prayer without such faith does not please God (Heb. 11:6), and no answer to it is to be expected.

In Mark 11:22-24, faith in prayer is said to refer not only to the nature of God, but to the certainty that what is asked in prayer will actually be granted. The questions that arise concerning the ground for faith in this sense are so important that it will be best to discuss them separately in the chapter on the content of prayer.[9]

E.   Obedience

There are a number of passages in which the efficacy of prayer is said to depend upon the "works" of the one who prays. Frequently in the Psalms the righteousness of the petitioner is given as a reason why his prayer should be heard: "Vindicate me, O Lord, for I have walked in my integrity . . ." (Ps. 26:1).

This cannot be dismissed as a sample of Old Testament legalism. Jesus singled out one petition of the Lord's Prayer for comment: "For if you forgive men their trespasses, your heavenly Father also will forgive you; but if you do not forgive men their trespasses, neither will your Father forgive your trespasses" (Matt. 6:14, 15; cf. Mark 11:25; Matt. 18:23-35). Here, one's willingness to forgive his brother is a condition for an answer to the prayer for forgiveness.

A similar condition is stated in I John 3:22: " . . . and we receive from him whatever we ask, because we keep his commandments and do what pleases him."

It might be concluded from these verses that answered prayer is a reward for the performance of acts of obedience. Upon closer examination, however, it is found that this is not the case. The context of I John 3:22 makes plain the relationship between obedience to God's commands and answered prayer. John has been discussing the command to love one another (I John 3:11). But such love is not the means of gaining God's favor, but the evidence that one already has received spiritual life from God: "We know that we have passed out of death into life, because we love the brethren" (I John 3:14). Obedience of the command to love is a result of union with Christ: "All who keep his commandments abide in him, and he in them" (I John 3:24). And only those who are thus united to Christ actually possess access to God, and therefore can pray with assurance that God will answer.

Obedience to the commands of God, willingness to forgive others are products, not causes of salvation. They are evidences of regeneration, by which men gain the right to call upon God as Father (cf. John 1:12, 13). When the saints mention their own righteousness in prayer, Calvin says, "By such expressions they mean nothing else but that by their regeneration itself they are attested as servants and children of God to whom he promises that he will be gracious."[10]

Thus it is appropriate to speak of obedience as a condition of prayer when obedience is understood as evidence of true *metanoia*, of a change of heart and will. Only the truly converted can pray efficaciously.

Just as repentance is inseparable from union with Christ, so all the subjective conditions for prayer must be viewed as gifts which Christ imparts to those who are his own.[11] Those who are in Christ Jesus are the sons of God through faith (Gal. 3:26); to those who are his children by virtue of their union with the Son, God has sent the Spirit of his Son, crying "Abba! Father!" (Gal. 4:6). And the Spirit works in them reverence, sincerity, submission, faith, obedience. These are not therefore conditions which are to be met by merely human effort, but are conditions which God himself graciously works in those who receive and rest upon Jesus Christ alone for their salvation.

chapter vii

the content of prayer

The practice of prayer recorded in Scripture, and the commands regarding it, indicate that while it is proper to use the forms of prayer given by inspiration, the content of prayer need not be limited to these. The apostolic church continued to use the Psalms in its worship (cf. Eph. 5:19); but prayer was not limited to these, nor to the actual form of the Lord's prayer.[1] There are many prayers which refer to specific historical situations: for example, the church's prayer for Peter when he was imprisoned (Acts 12:5), or Paul's prayer to be permitted to visit Rome (Rom. 1:9, 10). The command, "Have no anxiety about anything, but in everything by prayer and·supplication with thanksgiving let your requests be made known to God" (Phil. 4:6), indicates that the specific causes of anxiety in a person's life are to be made matters of prayer. Therefore prayer should not be limited to the use of fixed forms, even those given by inspiration.

Because the content of prayer is not restricted to the repetition of given forms, it must not be thought that there are no limits placed upon what may properly be asked of God in prayer.[2] It is true that some statements of Scripture seem at first glance to promise that God will answer any request at all that is made to him. Jesus said, "Ask, and it will be given you; seek, and you will find; knock, and it will be opened to you. For every one who asks receives, and he who seeks finds, and to him who knocks it will be opened" (Matt. 7:7, 8). However, such a statement must not be separated from its context, nor from the teaching of Scripture as a whole. It must be interpreted along with the Lord's Prayer, which is a part of the same discourse of Jesus. Whenever the promise is made that "anything" asked in prayer will be granted, the "anything" is qualified in one way or another. God will grant "anything" that is asked <u>in faith,</u> or <u>in the name of Christ,</u> or <u>in accordance with his will.</u> By considering the significance of these qualifying statements, the limits of the content of proper prayer will be made clear.

A.   The Content of Prayer Limited by Faith

The most significant passage in which faith appears as the condition of answered prayer is Mark 11:22-24: "And Jesus answered them, 'Have faith in God. Truly, I say to you, whoever says to this mountain, Be taken up and cast into the sea, and does not doubt in his heart, but believes that what he says will come to pass, it will be done for him. Therefore I tell you, whatever you ask in prayer, believe that you receive it, and you will' " (cf. Matt. 21:21, 22). By these words, Jesus indicated that results no less amazing than the immediate withering of the barren fig tree would be granted to prayer that is made in faith.

The content of prayer to which an answer is promised is left indefinite: *panta hosa proseuchesthe* - literally, "all things, as many as you pray" (Mark 11:24). The condition for the granting of prayer is *pisteuete hoti elabete* (Mark 11:24). *pisteuete* is in the present tense, while *elabete* is aorist, which means that the receiving is either prior to, or simultaneous with, the believing.[3] Thus Lenski translates, " . . . go on believing that you did receive them . . ."[4] Faith in this case means a confident expectation that what is asked will be granted, a certainty which does not waver.

The question immediately arises as to the basis for such confidence. The context makes it clear that the faith spoken of in Mark 11:24 is not sheer credulity, not a "leap in the dark," but has its ground in what is objectively true. The *pisteuete hoti elabete* of v. 24 must be taken with the *echete pistin theou* of v. 22. (*theou* is here the objective genitive, in accordance with the common New Testament usage).[5] Faith that prayer will be answered is inseparable from faith in the God who answers prayer.

Such faith, as has already been discussed, involves belief in God's ability and willingness to answer prayer. But it involves more: it is confidence also in the wisdom and the promise of God. One may believe in God's power and benevolence, and yet not be certain that a particular request will be granted, because he does not know whether it is according to God's will. Therefore the "faith in God" which makes it possible "to believe that you receive" is faith in God's promise, in the revelation which he has made of his will.

Jesus gives a specific example to show that the faith which expects an answer to prayer rests upon God's word of promise and command: the mountain being cast into the sea (Mark 11:23).

There is evidence that "moving a mountain" was a common metaphor for accomplishing the seemingly impossible. When Jesus used it on another occasion, he added, " . . . and nothing will be impossible to you" (Matt. 17:20). But Jesus was not speaking here of abstract possibility, but of what was actually to happen. As Hengstenberg has noted, the fig tree which was destroyed by Jesus' word was a symbol of the Jewish people, who face judgment because of their unbelief (cf. Luke 13:6-9).[6] In this connection, the mountain also has a symbolic meaning:

> "So the mountain here is the universal empire that then was, that of Rome. The sea is, according to the common symbolism of Scripture, the sea of nations . . . out of which the universal empire had arisen mightily in the time of its prosperity, but into which it now sinks back again through the faith of the disciples and the power of Christ."[7]

Thus faith for the casting down of the mountain had its basis in the revelation which promised the triumph of the kingdom of God - such as Daniel's interpretation of Nebuchadnezzar's vision: "But the stone that struck the image became a great mountain and filled the whole earth" (Dan. 2:35).

Mark 11:24, then, does not contain an unlimited promise that any prayer will be answered. The promise is qualified by faith, and faith is seen here to rest upon what has been revealed of God's nature and promise. As Lenski says,

> "Infidelic literalism may challenge a disciple to move a mountain or two and laugh when he is unable to do so; blind fanatics may tempt the Lord to fulfill his word, to do what that word never intended, and may even persuade themselves that their folly has come to pass. But neither of these affects the promise as it stands. God does no silly things, no useless things, none for mere display; yet it is his power that he places behind Jesus' disciples to do the things that he lays upon them as such disciples."[8]

Faith is not a belief that "anything can happen," but the confidence that <u>what God has promised will happen</u>. In accordance with this, the content of the prayer of faith is determined by what God has promised.

B.   The Content of Prayer Limited by the Will of God

Prayer with submission to God's will, and prayer according to God's will, are not precisely the same thing. In Gethsemane, Jesus prayed, " . . .not as I will, but as thou wilt" (Matt. 26:39), yet his petition, " . . . let this cup pass from me," was not according to his Father's will. Missing in this prayer of Jesus is the confident assurance that his request would be granted, which he expressed at other times (cf. John 11:41, 42).

In contrast to this is the promise of I John 5:14, 15: "And this is the confidence which we have in him, that if we ask anything according to his will he hears us. And if we know that he hears us in whatever we ask, we know that we have obtained the requests made of him." The most significant part of this statement is not that God hears (hearkens to, grants) prayers that are according to his will, but that a believer may know that his petition is heard, and therefore can be confident of the answer even before he actually experiences it. But since God acts in accordance with his own will (Eph. 1:11), such confidence can be present only if it is known that the prayer is according to God's will. The *thelēma* of God referred to here, then must be the revealed will of God.[9] John's meaning may be paraphrased as follows: "When you pray in accordance with God's revealed will, you can know with certainty that God will hear and answer your prayer."

It is clear that the knowledge of God's will has been given through the teaching of the prophets and apostles. It was the confidence of the Jews that in possessing the Law of Moses they knew the will of God (Rom. 2:17, 18). Jesus confirmed this when he compared them to a servant who knew his master's will (Luke 12:47). It was a part of Paul's apostolic commission to know God's will, and be a witness of what he had seen and heard (Acts 22:14, 15). Accordingly, those who received his instruction received knowledge of the will of God (I Thess. 4:1-3).

Not all of God's will has been revealed, and the hidden will of God also has significance for prayer;[10] but the positive teaching of I John 5:14, 15 is that the content of the prayer to which an answer can be confidently expected must conform to the revelation which God has given concerning his will.

C.   The Content of Prayer Limited by the Name of Christ

It is only necessary here to refer to the previous discussion of the meaning of the name of Christ,[11] in which it was shown that "the name of Christ" refers to the fullness of revelation regarding him. To pray in his name, then, involves not only faith in the revelation by which we know Jesus, but " . . . that the petition abide in the circle of that revelation."[12] Thus in John 14:13, "whatever you ask" is not unrestricted, but is governed by the phrase, "in my name." The promise of an answer is given only to prayer which is in harmony with the revelation which centers in Christ. Again, the content of prayer is regulated by the Word of God.

The freedom from fixed forms in prayer, then, is not unlimited freedom. Whenever the promise is given that God will hear and answer the prayers of his people, the condition is either implied or explicitly stated, "if they are according to the Word of God." Probably no one has stressed this intimate connection between the Word of God and prayer more than Calvin. He says, "Again, only out of faith is God pleased to be called upon, and he expressly bids that prayers be conformed to the measure of his Word. Finally, faith grounded upon the Word is the mother of right prayer; hence as soon as it is deflected from the Word, prayer must needs be corrupted."[13] Calvin regards the Lord's Prayer as the summary of Scriptural teaching about what may be asked in prayer. Therefore,

> " . . . those who dare go farther and ask anything from God beyond this: first, wish to add to God's wisdom from their own, which cannot happen without insane blasphemy; secondly, do not confine themselves within God's will but, holding it in contempt, stray away farther in their uncontrolled desire; lastly, they will never obtain anything, since they pray without faith . . . for here the word of God is absent, upon which faith, if it is to stand at all, must always rely."[14]

Every proper prayer must be capable of being related to the petitions of the Lord's Prayer.[15]

D. Degrees of Conformity to the Word of God in Prayer

Three classes of prayers may be distinguished in relation to the principle that the content of prayer is to be regulated by the Word of God, and corresponding to them, three different kinds of expectancy are possible.

1. There is, first of all, prayer which rests upon explicit commands and promises of Scripture. When a person prays for the forgiveness of sin, he has the command of Christ to pray like this: "And forgive us our debts . . . (Matt. 6:12), and the promise of John: "If we confess our sins, he is faithful and just, and will forgive our sins and cleanse us from all unrighteousness" (I John 1:9). James 1:5 authorizes prayer for wisdom: "If any of you lacks wisdom, let him ask God . . ." In such cases, there can be no ques-

tion that the request is according to the will of God. Therefore, a confident expectation that an answer will be given is justified, is in fact required. To have any doubt in such prayers is to reject the truth of God's Word. In prayer of this kind, as Calvin says, "If we would pray fruitfully, we ought therefore to grasp with both hands this assurance of obtaining what we ask . . ."[16]

2.   A second kind of prayer is that which is known to be in harmony with the Word of God in its intent, but in which the specific features of the request have no explicit basis in Scripture. These are specific requests which rest upon general promises of Scripture. For example, we are commanded to pray for daily bread (Matt. 6:11), and God promises to supply the necessities of life (Matt. 6:30, 33). Therefore one can be confident in praying that his needs will be supplied, and yet not be certain that a particular felt need (which may not be really necessary) will be met in answer to prayer. To give another example from Scripture: Paul felt that it would be in harmony with the furthering of the kingdom of God if he were to visit Rome, and so he prayed that he might be able to do so (Rom. 1:9, 10). Yet he had no revelation from God that it was actually God's will that he go there at that time. So he indicates some uncertainty in his prayer - "by God's will" in this case means, "if it really is God's will." God's will has been revealed in its essentials, but not in all its details: "It is not for you to know times or seasons . . ." (Acts 1:7). "Therefore," Calvin says, "where no certain promise shows itself, we must ask of God conditionally."[17] Prayers about specific events and times and persons, in the absence of specific promises, must always include the proviso "If the Lord wills . . ." (James 4:15). Confidence in such cases rests in the fact that God will accomplish his purpose in wisdom and love, not that a specific request will be granted. Otherwise, there would be the danger of presuming to control God, to bind him to man's will. In the Lord's Prayer, according to Calvin, " . . . we are taught not to make any law for him, or impose any condition upon him, but to leave to his decision to do what he is to do, in what way, at what time, and in what place it seems good to him."[18]

3.   A third class of prayer is that which has no basis at all in Scripture. James referred to this kind of prayer when he wrote, "You ask and do not receive, because you ask wrongly, to spend it on your passions" (James 4:3). All of the preceding discussion goes

to show that in such prayers there is no justification for expecting an answer. Instead, they provoke God's wrath, as is illustrated by the history of Israel: "But they soon forgot his works; they did not wait for his counsel. But they had a wanton craving in the wilderness, and put God to the test in the desert; he gave them what they asked, but sent a wasting disease among them" (Ps. 106:13-15).

There is a special kind of prayer which seems to belong to this category of prayer that lacks a foundation in the Word of God: the prayer of doubt and complaint. When Job prays, "Does it seem good to thee to oppress, to despise the work of thy hands and favor the designs of the wicked?" (Job 10:3), he seems to lack faith in God's justice and benevolence. Of course, not every prayer recorded in Scripture is a model which is to be emulated, but the fact that the Psalms, which believers are authorized to use in worship (Col. 3:16), contain expressions of doubt, indicates that such prayers are not always improper. There are a number of reasons why this is so.

First, when believers actually do experience doubt, when they are puzzled about God's dealing with them, it is better to express their real feelings to God than not to pray at all, or to pretend that they have no such feelings. It is to encourage weak Christians to pray that the assurance is given concerning the sympathy of Christ as our high priest (Heb. 4:15, 16). The prayer of doubt is not necessarily devoid of all faith. It is a recognition that God exists, and that he knows the thoughts of the heart. In his trouble, the believer does not turn away from God, but turns to him, in the kind of prayer which Kuyper calls the "outpouring of the soul."[19]

Secondly, it is not inconsistent with true faith in God's mercy to be conscious of God's displeasure. In his love, God chastens and disciplines his children (Heb. 12:6). Therefore it may well be that for a time his favor is withheld, and his anger is felt. At such times it is appropriate for the believer to pray, "There is no soundness in my flesh because of thy indignation; there is no health in my bones because of my sin" (Ps. 38:3). At the same time, there is confidence in God's mercy, and a plea for restoration of his favor: "Make haste to help me, O Lord, my salvation!" (Ps. 38:22).

Finally, in almost every case, in the Psalms, the expression of doubt represents a preliminary stage in prayer - the statement of need. Eventually, there is not only a plea for help, but praise for the answer that has been given. Ps. 73 is an example of such a progression.

The prayer of doubt and complaint has its place, then, in so far as it is an honest expression to God of one's inner state, and represents a way of presenting one's need to God and seeking his help. Even though all the sentiments expressed may not harmonize with what is revealed in Scripture, such prayer has for its basis the Scriptural truth that the Lord " . . . will regard the prayer of the destitute, and will not despise their supplication" (Ps. 102:17).

chapter VIII

the summary of the doctrine of prayer

On the basis of the preceding study of the teaching of the Scriptures regarding prayer, the following conclusions are set forth as the substance of the Christian doctrine of prayer:

1.   Prayer is speech addressed by man to God. It springs from man's consciousness of the relationship in which he stands to God, and is the means by which he expresses the affections, needs, and desires which arise from that relationship. As such, it includes adoration and thanksgiving, confession of sin, submission, commitment, and petition.

2.   God is not addressed as though he were a man, nor should man be addressed as though he were God. Prayer is therefore to be made to God alone. Because God exists in three Persons, prayer may be addressed to the Triune God, without further specification, or to each of the Persons. The Father, however, has a distinctive role as the Hearer of prayer, and prayer is ordinarily to be addressed to him.

3.   By his sin, man is estranged from God, and unable to hold intercourse with him in prayer. By his high priestly work, Jesus Christ has made expiation for the sins of his people, and thereby has given them access to the presence of God in prayer. He continues to act as high priest in making intercession for the saints, pleading before the throne of God for their full salvation, and powerfully succouring them in all their needs. Although believers before his Advent did not enjoy as clear a knowledge of his mediatorial work, nor as full an experience of the working of the Holy Spirit, access to God in all ages has been possible by virtue of his once offering himself as a sacrifice for sins.

4.   Prayer is impossible for the unredeemed sinner, not only because he is barred from God's presence, but because he lacks the motivation and knowledge necessary to pray aright. The Holy Spirit works in the lives of the redeemed to destroy the power of

sin, and to enable them to pray, by giving them spiritual understanding, faith, and love for God and men. Because this work of renewal is not yet complete, the Spirit also assists believers in their weakness by making intercession within them according to the will of God.

5.   As a recipient of the grace of God, the Christian exhibits in his practice of prayer the qualities of reverence toward the majesty and holiness of God, sincerity and earnestness, submission to the will of God, faith in what God has revealed concerning himself and his activity in the world, and obedience to God's commands. These qualities do not merit God's response to prayer, but are evidence that the one possessing them is a child of God, to whom he has given the promise of answered prayer.

6.   God's sovereign will is not subject to control or change by man, and therefore God's promise to answer prayer is qualified by the revelation which he has given of his will in Scripture. To pray efficaciously, one must pray according to what God has promised and commanded in Scripture. Confidence that an answer will be given to prayer is dependent upon the assurance that what is asked has been promised in the Word of God.

7.   The efficacy of prayer does not rest in itself, as though it had some magical power, nor in its subjective effect upon the one who prays. The effects of right prayer are produced by the response of God, who controls all events in the world, who can do all things, who acts in accordance with the counsel of his will, and who hears and answers the prayers of his people.

These conclusions present no finding that can be called new. This is not to say that the practice and teaching of prayer within the Church of the present day conforms to these truths. In particular, the close connection between the content of prayer and the revelation given in the Scriptures is often ignored even within evangelical Christianity. Calvin's strong emphasis upon the fact that prayer must be within the limits of the Word of God, and that the faith which expects an answer to prayer must have its basis in the revelation which God has given of his will, needs to be given new prominence at the present time. In accordance with this, the Church needs to recapture its historical emphasis upon the Lord's Prayer as the paradigm for all prayer. Not only should teaching about prayer be based upon it, but great benefits could be derived from making the Lord's Prayer the structural basis for both private and public prayer. That is to say, in addition to using the Lord's Prayer as an actual form of prayer, its phrases may be used as the foci around which the expressions and petitions of free prayer are gathered.

Without claiming to have penetrated fully into the way in which the prayers of finite men influence the course of events which is absolutely controlled by the sovereign God, this study has shown that prayer has a place of primary importance in individual piety, and in the accomplishment of God's purpose in the world. Not because God cannot work unless men pray, but because he has commanded men to pray, and promises to answer the prayer of faith, men whose lives are governed by God's Word and Spirit will be men who pray.

chapter ix

the defense of prayer

While seeking to give a positive presentation of Scriptural teaching regarding prayer, a theological discussion of prayer must also deal with the objections which have been raised against it. The objections have been many and varied, but the most important of them call into question either the necessity of prayer, or else its efficacy. Generally speaking, the question about the necessity of prayer arises within the framework of belief in the Scriptures, while denial of the efficacy of prayer is the fruit of unbelief.

A. The Necessity of Prayer

"Objection" may be too strong a word to describe the kind of questioning which arises in the minds of believers about the necessity of prayer. It is a matter of seeking to reconcile what the Scripture teaches about prayer with its revelation about the nature of God. If God is infinitely wise and benevolent; if it is true that " . . . your Father knows what you need before you ask him" (Matt. 6:8), if he " . . . is able to do far more abundantly than all we ask or think . . ." (Eph. 3:20), then what good does it do to pray? Will not God do what is best for us whether we ask him or not?

There are not many who, on the basis of this question, deliberately adopt the position that prayer is to be abandoned. In so far as their faith in God's wisdom and benevolence is genuine, they are impelled to obey God's command that men are to pray, and so they do. Nevertheless, the intellectual problem remains, and no doubt it often has the effect of making prayer more formal and less urgent than it ought to be.

The Scripture nowhere deals directly with this question; it does not explain why God, who knows what his people need and is willing to give it to them, commands them to pray for these needs. The fact remains that he does command men to pray, promises to respond when they pray, and indicates that if they do not pray they will not receive (James 4:2). The command to pray is found side by side with the statement that God already knows our needs, and will supply them (cf. Matt. 6:8-13, 32, 33; 7:7, 8).

Still, men seek reasons why prayer is necessary. One that is commonly advocated, and that seems to give prayer great urgency, is the view that while God is ready and willing to bless men, he cannot unless by prayer they indicate their willingness for him to do so. S. D. Gordon, a popular evangelical writer on prayer at the turn of the century, gives such an explanation: "Everything that has ever been prayed for, of course I mean every right thing, God has already purposed to do. But He does nothing without our consent. He has been hindered in His purpose by our lack of willingness. When we learn His purposes and make them our prayers we are giving Him an opportunity to act."[1]

Such an explanation makes prayer necessary in the absolute sense - it is something which God cannot do without. Unless men pray, he is unable to accomplish his benevolent purpose in the world. The progress of God's kingdom in the world, and the eternal destiny of individuals is ultimately dependent upon the human activity of prayer.[2]

While this kind of an explanation of the necessity of prayer has a strong psychological and emotional appeal, its implications are devastating. It denies the sovereign control of God over his creation and makes events to rest upon the free will of finite sinful men. If the purpose and activity of God did not control events, then all human activity would be meaningless, including prayer. Since many men are involved, all acting as free agents, what was accomplished through the prayer of one could be negated by the failure of many others to pray. It would be just as likely - more so, because men's wills are "warped and weakened" - that God's purpose would fail as that it would succeed, and hence all prayer would come to nothing.

The Scriptures present a far different view of the relation between the purpose of God and human will. God " . . . does according to his will in the host of heaven and among the inhabitants of the earth; and none can stay his hand or say to him, 'What doest thou?' " (Dan. 4:35). "A man's mind plans his way, but the Lord directs his steps" (Prov. 16:9). " . . . God is at work in you, both to will and to work for his good pleasure" (Phil. 2:13). Such passages indicate that God's purpose is sovereign, and that man's will is subject to it. The impulse and ability to pray come from God. Thus prayer cannot be said to be absolutely necessary in the sense that events are ultimately determined by it.

Instead, the necessity of prayer is a relative one; it is necessary because it is one of the means by which God is pleased to accomplish his purpose. And it is not difficult to discern the benefits which accrue to believers by virtue of the fact that God chooses to grant his blessings to them in answer to prayer. Calvin suggests six: (1) quickening of our love for God; (2) purification of our desires; (3) stimulation of gratitude; (4) greater appreciation of the kindness of God; (5) greater delight in the blessings received; (6) greater confidence in God's promises.[3]

A belief in God's sovereignty can itself create problems in understanding the necessity of prayer. If God has unchangeably foreordained whatever happens, then how can prayer have any significance? Since God has declared the end from the beginning, and infallibly accomplishes his purpose (Isa. 46:10), then prayer cannot change his plan. Prayer seems, then, to be superfluous.

This kind of question is only a part of the larger problem of the relation between the sovereignty of God and the significance of all human activity. It is just as easy to conclude from the foreordination of God that believing in Christ, or preaching the gospel, or attempting to safeguard oneself from physical harm, accomplishes nothing, as to say that prayer has no effect.

The solution to the dilemma is not to be found by giving to prayer, or any other human activity, a significance and value which is independent of God's plan and activity. If man's will is regarded as independent from God, then, as has been said, there could be no assurance that prayer would be answered, since God might be confronted with the impregnable resistance of human will. As John Murray has pointed out, if man were able to command " . . . a realm impervious to God's providence, then there would be a realm which his grace could not invade."[4]

Human activity appears in Scripture, not as the complement or antithesis of divine activity, but as the means by which God's purposes are carried out. In his discussion of providence, Calvin links praying with man's planning for the future and taking precautions against accident and disease, which the profane say are useless since God's plan is already fixed.[5] Calvin repudiates such a view: "These fools do not consider what is under their very eyes, that the Lord has inspired in men the arts of taking counsel and caution, by which to comply with his providence in the preservation of life itself."[6] So God moves men to pray in order that he may respond to their prayers, and thus carry out his will. God ordains means as well as ends, and it is this which gives prayer its meaning.

Paul finds no contradiction between prayer and God's eternal decree. In his most extended discussion of predestination, where he shows that the salvation or rejection of Israel rests upon God's purpose of election (Rom. 9-11), he can say, "Brethren, my heart's desire and prayer to God for them is that they may be saved" (Rom. 10:1). He is confident that God will complete the work of salvation which he has begun in the Philippians (Phil. 1:6; cf. Rom. 8:29-30); and what he is sure God will do, he prays for (Phil. 1:9-11).

Without attempting to achieve perfect comprehension of the relation between God's sovereignty and human activity,[7] the believer must hold firmly to what is revealed in Scripture, namely that while God " . . . accomplishes all things according to the counsel of his will . . ." (Eph. 1:11), he also responds to the prayer of his people who pray in accordance with his will. To conclude from God's sovereignty that prayer is unnecessary is to reason contrary to the clear teaching of the Word of God.

B.   The Efficacy of Prayer

In much of recent theological writing about prayer, there is a strong defensive note. It is as though the question were being asked, "Is it still possible to pray?" - with the implication that recent developments in human knowledge have made the practice of prayer, especially petitionary prayer, very questionable. As Heiler says in his famous work on prayer, "For modern thought, dominated by Copernicus and Kant, prayer is as great a stone of stumbling as it was for the enlightened philosophy of the Greeks."[8]

In many cases the attempt is made to salvage some meaning for prayer while accepting the non-biblical presuppositions of modern thought. It will be the purpose of this section to discuss two of the forms in which the modern attack on prayer has been made; the way in which these attacks have been answered on the basis of modern thought; and then to evaluate the answers from a Biblical prespective.

1.   Objections from the Standpoint of Natural Law

In the nineteenth and early twentieth century, many writers on prayer felt it necessary to defend prayer in the face of a prevalent world view which held that all events were determined by the operation of fixed and unchanging natural laws. Charles Hodge devoted more space to this question than to any other in his treatment of prayer.[9] George Buttrick wrote his book on prayer " . . . in a silent protest against yielding to an unexamined concept of natural law."[10]

A book by William Adams Brown offers a very clear presentation of the difficulty for prayer posed by "natural law," and a way of meeting the difficulty that is characteristic of the older liberalism.[11]

Brown states the problem in this way:

"There is, first of all, the difficulty which grows out of the new conception of the world which science has given us. What room is there in our world of law, where effect follows cause in inexorable sequence, for the direct initiative of God which the saints take for granted? If there be a God at all, is it not reasonable to suppose that he has expressed himself adequately in the laws he has made? What ground have we, then, for thinking that our prayer can make any difference in his activity?"[12]

While Brown acknowledges that this view of a closed universe of unalterable law is open to question, he assumes its truth for the purpose of his argument, because many people are convinced that it is true.[13]

One possible solution is to suggest that man, even though he himself is completely determined, nevertheless has the experience of creative freedom. That is, he can to an extent manipulate the laws of nature so as to solve his problems and shape his world. And if man can do that, why not God?

"World of law though it may be, ours is a world in which new things are constantly coming to pass . . . In countless ways we fashion the raw materials of our world after patterns which our minds conceive. Why, then, should we conclude that man alone possesses this capacity? Shall the power that produced man be less resourceful than the creature it has produced?"[14]

Still, it cannot be confidently asserted that prayers are answered " . . . in the way our fathers believed they were answered . . ."[15] - that is, by God's special intervention in the world.

The main thrust of Brown's argument lies in another direction. Prayer, for him, is not primarily petition, but is " . . . the practice of the presence of God."[16] Prayer is not intended to have any influence upon God, but gives insight into ultimate values and order. Practicing the presence of God " . . . does not mean that we are to put pressure upon God to come where he is not. It means, rather, that we should concentrate our thought on those aspects of life which assure us that he is here already."[17]

In terms of the psychology on which Brown depends, the elements of human personality tend to be in a state of confusion and conflict. In order to restore health, these conflicting elements must be unified by being attached to a higher principle, something which provides a motive, standard, and goal for human life. God serves as such a principle of integration for the praying man. "Prayer brings us into contact with God, and God is the only object in the world big enough and lasting enough and worthy enough to serve as the integrating principle of every human personality."[18]

In prayer, God is experienced as the unifying principle, not only of the individual, but of the universe. In prayer one finds freedom from doubt and fear, because he sees a fundamental order and beauty and goodness in the universe which would otherwise be a threat to him.[19]

Since in prayer a person finds harmony with himself and the world, he is changed, and this change has repercussions in the lives of others. It is thus that one may account for the value of intercessory prayer. "We lose the true significance of intercessory prayer if we think of it as the means by which we bring to God those for whom we should pray. Rather, it is God's means of revealing to us what he desires for others, so that we can pray for them aright."[20] In prayer for others, one gains insight into their real needs, and his attitude toward them is changed, so that he goes out to serve them. The wider results of prayer are traceable to the enlightenment which comes to the one who prays.

Does such an account of prayer describe anything more than a process of auto-suggestion? Brown answers that it is indeed auto-suggestion, but that while the unbelieving psychologist concludes that prayer is a delusion, the man of faith sees in the process of auto-suggestion the working of God.

"In prayer we experience genuine creation: new values arise and new appreciations of old values. Granted that we ourselves are the creators of these values and of these appreciations, who is it that made us what we are? . . . In prayer we become aware of God at work . . ."[21]

To summarize, Brown sees God as related to the world in terms of purposeful activity. There is order and progress in God's working, so that the world moves in the direction of unity in which presently conflicting elements will be brought into harmony. In prayer, man gains insight into the unity which lies beyond the present disorder, and so achieves integration of his own personality and a harmonious relation to the world. This enables him to see others in a new light, and to act for their welfare. Prayer thus has a social as well as an individual effect. Whether prayer has any objective result beyond this remains doubtful.

Brown's attempt to give a defense for prayer while accepting the view that events in the world are determined by "natural" causes which are not subject to change by God must be judged a failure. From Brown's own standpoint, if the effect of prayer in the world is due to auto-suggestion, then there is no reason why, for example, the voicing of one's hopes and aspirations should not serve just as well as speech which takes the form of prayer. Prayer might still "work" for the unenlightened, but Brown is writing for those who are seeking an intellectual basis for the practice of prayer. Surely if they understand Brown's reasoning, they will conclude that prayer, in its petitionary form, does not work. Rather, prayer is reduced to "the practice of the presence of God," that is, contemplation or meditation. And petition is unnecessary, and really inappropriate, in meditation.

But, more seriously, Brown's explanation of prayer ignores, or contradicts, the Biblical view of prayer.[22] It cannot account for Scriptural assertions that prayer can produce effects in the forces of nature, as in the case of Elijah's prayer for rain (James 5:18). Nor can it explain how, for example, Paul could anticipate that through the prayers of people in Philippi he would be freed from prison in distant Rome (Phil. 1:19). The Biblical claim that prayer can have results in the physical world, and in the lives of people at a distance, rests upon the reality of the response and activity of the God who is the creator and governor of all causes and effects.

Against the attacks of a "scientific" world view which sees " . . . an uninterrupted natural interdependence between all things and the absolute dominion of the law of cause and effect . . .",[23] the defense of prayer requires the maintenance of a Biblical doctrine of providence. Such a doctrine does not regard anything in the world as independent of God. Abraham Kuyper rejected a dichotomy between "natural" and "supernatural," " . . . as though nature is a power that stands over against God with its own forces and laws . . ."[24] There is no question of whether God can affect the forces of nature, for those forces are the work of God. Because there is order and regularity in God's working, it is possible to speak of "natural laws." But they are laws of God's appointment, which offer no resistance when he works in new and unusual ways.

When this Biblical teaching regarding God's providential activity is accepted, then the attack upon prayer from the standpoint of a "scientific world view" is successfully refuted.

2.   Objection Based upon the Denial that God is Personal

In a recent book on prayer, P. R. Baelz has noted the disagreement which exists in contemporary Christendom over the appropriateness of personal terminology in speaking of God: "Christian tradition makes liberal use of the personal language of divine activity and purpose. Reflection on the mysterious being of God compels us to ask whether such language is to be taken seriously or whether it expresses a lingering but persistent anthropomorphism which needs to be radically discounted."[25] For a large part of modern theology, the latter alternative has been chosen. Yet, inasmuch as there is still a desire to live and think within the framework of the Christian Church, and since prayer has always been a central part of Christian worship, an attempt is made to give a meaningful account of how prayer "works."

One such attempt is found in the systematic theology of John Macquarrie, a professor, like Brown, at Union Theological Seminary in New York.[26] Macquarrie takes the thought of Martin Heidegger as the philosophical framework of his theology,[27] and thus attempts to interpret God as "Being." God is not a being among others, nor is he (it?) a cause or some kind of basic "stuff" which underlies the world; rather, God is " . . . the condition that there may be any beings or properties of beings . . ."[28] "Being" is that which "lets be."[29] Hence the man of faith is one who takes "an existential attitude of acceptance and commitment" toward the "letting-be" of "Being."[30]

Within such a framework, prayer cannot be the address of a human person to a divine Person; "Being" is not conscious, and is not capable of acts of will. " . . . we cannot suppose that prayer is a kind of conversation between man and God or that the usual conditions for communication can obtain in this case . ."[31] Hence prayer becomes " . . the way by which we can give shape to our deepest desires, aspirations, and concerns, and, as it were, hold them up in the presence of holy Being . ."[32] This exposure of inward desires has a purifying effect, as some of those desires is seen to be unworthy.[33]

But prayer works positively as well as negatively. "Petitionary prayer makes sense if we are committing ourselves to what we are praying for . . ."[34] The effect of prayer is not only psychological:

> "It seems to me that without falling into any magical or fanciful notions on the subject, one may readily admit that prayer has repercussions beyond the life of the person or persons who actually offer the prayer. Let us think for a moment of the prayer for the coming of the kingdom. While on the one hand this prayer may be a strengthening of one's own commitment to Christ's kingdom, may we not also believe that the sincere prayer of faith is a strengthening of the movement of Being itself in its threefold action of creation-reconciliation-consummation? For this, as we have seen, is not something that proceeds just automatically, but something that needs man's free response and cooperation."[35]

Man, by his prayer, actually shares in the "letting-be" of Being, and thus changes are produced in the world. Petitionary prayer, by this account, becomes primarily an act of commitment by which one participates in the process of the ever greater realization of existence.

A similar view is advocated by Robert Simpson, who has investigated the writings of five of the Fathers on the Lord's Prayer, with the purpose of obtaining guidelines for a restatement of the doctrine of prayer.[36]

Drawing upon " . . . the emerging tradition of process thought,"[37] Simpson regards the concept of God as a symbol for "creative activity", which is " . . . that process by which more complex forms of related-being are produced. That is, creative activity is the increasing integration of divergent elements."[38] It involves both biological evolution and the development of inter-personal relations. Faith is essentially, "the acknowledgement of the significance of this process as the ultimate value in human life and the consequent commitment to it . . ."[39] The process of increasing integration is enhanced and forwarded by the free participation in it on the part of human beings.

Within such a framework, Simpson defines prayer as " . . . that expression of religion which involves a conscious orientation toward creative activity at the human level by which participation in that activity is facilitated."[40]

The key word in this definition is "orientation." As orientation, prayer involves a struggle of wills in which the will of the individual is conformed to the integrative process. Since the orientation is to "creative activity at the human level," it is orientation to the community.[41] It is not conformity to a transcendent will of God, but to the life of the community of which one is a part, in so far as that life moves toward more complete integration.

Prayer is an orientation of will, and as such involves commitment. It is not mere "willingness," but a decision to participate. Therefore, prayer " . . . gives that which it seeks . . . The ideal of Christian prayer involves ultimate commitment and conscious orientation to creative activity through which ultimate human values are realized."[42]

Like Brown, Simpson does not shrink before the charge that prayer is auto-suggestion. " 'Auto-suggestion' may be said to describe one means by which creative activity occurs, as the means by which the ultimate Source of truth, beauty, and value operates at the human level, only if the term is redefined to mean a fresh integration of values and meanings (and power) that are previously present but inadequately related."[43]

Such a view of prayer does not regard God as personal in the sense that he would respond to prayer in an objective way apart from the change of orientation in the one who prays. " . . . Christian prayer aims not at the conformity of certain powers to human purposes but at the conformity of man to the demands or conditions by which higher degrees of related being may be achieved . . ."[44] God is the "transcendent Referrent" of prayer in the sense that creative activity is both the object of ultimate commitment and also the ground or source of prayer. Prayer arises from creative activity and is commitment to creative activity.[45]

Both Macquarrie and Simpson attempt to reinterpret Christian prayer in terms of modern world-views which do not claim to have their basis in the revelation of God in Scripture. Prayer is understood by both to be basically an act of commitment to the movement of being, a movement which is either in the direction of more complete existence (Macquarrie), or of a higher degree of integration (Simpson).

It is certainly true that prayer can express commitment. Jesus' words from the cross, "Father, into thy hands I commit my spirit!" (Luke 23:46) was such a prayer. But to make commitment the essence of prayer is to nullify the Biblical teaching about prayer, and makes meaningless much of the language of prayer as it has been practiced by the Christian Church through the centuries. If God is not a word that refers to "a being," then it is absurd to use terms of personal address in prayer. If there is no Person to respond to prayer, then it is senseless to voice petitions such as those which make up the Lord's Prayer. If prayer is essentially an act of commitment, then the language of most Christian prayer is at best a clumsy circumlocution. If men like Macquarrie and Simpson are right, then the prayers of the Psalter and even the Lord's Prayer ought to disappear from the Church's worship, to be replaced by something only analogous to prayer.

The teaching about prayer in the Bible cannot be separated from the Biblical view of God and the world which is its foundation and context. The defense of Christian prayer cannot be successfully undertaken apart from an acceptance of the Biblical revelation as a whole. But when man by faith apprehends God as personal, conscious, active, powerful, and benevolent; when he sees the world as created by God, and under God's sovereign control; when he embraces the commands and promises of God concerning prayer as set forth in the Scriptures; then prayer in all its aspects, not excluding petition, becomes a reasonable and meaningful practice.

footnotes

INTRODUCTION

[1] Charles Hodge, Conference Papers (New York: Charles Scribner's Sons, 1879), p. 293.

[2] For the teaching of five of the Fathers on the Lord's Prayer, vide Robert L. Simpson, The Interpretation of Prayer in the Early Church (Philadelphia: The Westminster Press, [1965]).

[3] Quoted in George A. Buttrick, Prayer (New York and Nashville: Abingdon-Cokesbury Press, [1942]), p. 16.

[4] S. D. Gordon, Quiet Talks on Prayer (New York: Fleming H. Revell Company, [1904]).

[5] Ibid., p. 43.

[6] Ibid., p. 81.

[7] A more extensive discussion of the difficulties alluded to is given in chap. IX.

[8] John Calvin, Institutes of the Christian Religion, bk. III, chap. XX. Hereafter cited as Institutes, with the numbers of the book, chapter, and section. Quotations are from vols. XX and XXI of The Library of Christian Classics, ed. by John T. McNeill, trans. by Ford Lewis Battles (Philadelphia: The Westminster Press, [1960]).

[9] Infra, pp. 53, 66ff.

[10] Heinrich Heppe, Reformed Dogmatics, trans. by G. T. Thomson (London: George Allen and Unwin, 1950).

[11] The Westminster Confession of Faith, chap. XXI; Larger Catechism, quest. 154; Shorter Catechism, quest. 88, in The Constitution of the Reformed Presbyterian Church of North America (Pittsburgh: The Synod of the Reformed Presbyterian Church, [1949]), pp. 37, 38, 111, 144. Added on Copies 1 & 2 (Contains the corrected text of the Confession of Faith edited by S. W. Carruthers).

[12] John Dick, Lectures on Theology, II (New York: Robert Carter and Brothers, 1868), pp. 423-453.

[13] Charles Hodge, Systematic Theology, III (Grand Rapids, Mich.: Wm. B. Eerdmans Publishing Company, 1958), pp. 692-709;

[14] Abraham Kuyper, The Work of the Holy Spirit, trans. by

Henri de Vries (New York and London: Funk and Wagnalls Company, 1900), pp. 618-649.

15 John Owen, "A Discourse of the Work of the Holy Spirit in Prayer," in The Works of John Owen, IV, ed. by William Goold (London and Edinburgh: Johnstone and Hunter, 1852), pp. 236-338.

16 Some examples of contemporary treatments of prayer are given in chap. IX.

17 Abraham Kuyper, Principles of Sacred Theology, trans. by J. Hendrick de Vries (Grand Rapids, Mich.: Wm. B. Eerdmans Publishing Company, 1965), pp. 341ff.

CHAPTER I   The Definition of Prayer

1 Maurice Nedoneelle, The Nature and Use of Prayer, trans. by A. Manson (London: Burns & Oates, 1964), analyses petition addressed to other men as a basis for the study of petition addressed to God.

2 Scripture quotations in the thesis, unless otherwise noted, are from the Revised Standard Version (New York: Thomas Nelson and Sons, 1953). Quotations from the Greek text of the New Testament are from Nestle's 24th ed. (Stuttgart, 1960).

3 Cf. Abraham Kuyper, The Work of the Holy Spirit, pp. 620ff.

CHAPTER II   The Old Testament Background

1 Vide Abraham Kuyper, Principles of Sacred Theology, pp. 473ff.

2 A helpful survey of prayer in the Old Testament (though characterized by acceptance of "higher critical" views) is given by Johannes Herrmann, in Gerhard Kittel, ed., Theological Dictionary of the New Testament, trans. and ed. by Geoffrey W. Bromiley, II (Grand Rapids, Mich.: Wm. B. Eerdmans Publishing Company, 1964), pp. 785-800. Hereafter, this work is cited as TDNT.

3 The Book of Job, which narrates events from the age of the patriarchs, exhibits an understanding of prayer which rests on such a basis.

4 Cf. TDNT, II, p. 790.

5 Isaac Watts defended the introduction of his hymns into the worship of the church by asserting the unsuitability of Old Testament Psalms for use as Christian praise: "While we are kindling into Divine Love by the Meditations of the loving Kindness of God, and the Multitude of his tender Mercies, within a few Verses some dreadful

Curse against Men is propos'd to our Lips . . . which is . . . contrary to the New Commandment, of loving our Enemies . . ." Selma L. Bishop, Isaac Watts: Hymns and Spiritual Songs 1707-1748 (London: The Faith Press, 1962), p. lii.

[6] Imprecatory prayer is not absent from the New Testament. The souls of martyrs are portrayed as praying, "O Sovereign Lord, holy and true, how long before thou wilt judge and avenge our blood on those who dwell upon the earth?" (Rev. 6:10). Since the Second Coming of Christ is for the judgment of the wicked as well as for the salvation of his people (Matt. 25:31-46), Christians pray for the destruction of the wicked when they pray, "Come, Lord Jesus!" (Rev. 22:20).

[7] Infra, pp. 53ff.

[8] TDNT, II, p. 794.

[9] Vide Patrick Fairbairn, The Typology of Scripture, I (Philadelphia: Daniels and Smith, 1852) pp. 52-68.

CHAPTER III   The Object of Prayer

[1] Supra, p. 10.

[2] For a discussion of the role of faith in prayer, vide infra, pp. 78ff.

[3] Calvin says, "And truly God claims, and would have us grant him, omnipotence—not the empty, idle, and almost unconscious sort that the Sophists imagine, but a watchful, effective, active sort, engaged in ceaseless activity." Institutes, I: XVI: 3.

[4] Cf. chap. IX.

[5] The Second Helvetic Confession, chap. V, in Arthur C. Cochrane, ed., Reformed Confessions of the 16th Century (Philadelphia, The Westminster Press, [1966]), p. 231.

[6] H. J. Schroeder, Canons and Decrees of the Council of Trent (St. Louis, Mo. and London: B. Herder Book Company 1941), p. 215.

[7] "Then who, whether angel or demon, ever revealed to any man even a syllable of the kind of saint's intercessions they invent? For there is nothing about it in Scripture . . . Surely, when human wit is always seeking after assistance for which we have no support in God's Word, it clearly reveals its own faithlessness." John Calvin, Institutes, III: XX: 21.

[8] Ibid., III: XX: 22.

[9] Schroeder, op.cit., p. 216.

[10] Vide "Beatification and Canonization," in The Catholic Encyclopedia, II (New York: Robert Appleton Company, [1907]), pp. 364ff.

[11] Institutes, III: XX: 22.

[12] Paul Tillich, Systematic Theology, III (Chicago: The University of Chicago Press, 1963), p. 289.

[13] The term erōtaō is used, especially in John, for the prayer of Christ to the Father, because of Christ's unique relationship with the Father, in which he asks "upon equal terms." Vide R. C. Trench, Synonyms of the New Testament, (12th ed.; London: Kegan Paul, Trench, Trubner and Company, 1894), p. 145.

[14] "Martha . . . reveals her poor unworthy conception of his person, that she recognizes in Him no more than a prophet, when she ascribes that aiteisthai to Him, which He never ascribes to Himself: hosa an aitēsē ton theon, dōsei soi ho theos." Idem.

[15] Although a different word is used, prayer is described as a "coming" to God in Heb. 4:16.

[16] Nestle (24th ed.) gives it as the preferred reading. It is found in the Codex Sinaiticus and the Codex Vaticanus, and is supported by the Vulgate.

[17] The verb aitēsēte, with Jesus as the object, is used in the same sense as in John 16:23, where the Father is the object.

[18] Institutes, I: XIII: 5.

[19] Institutes, I: XIII: 17.

[20] Calvin says, " . . . whenever the name of God is mentioned without particularization, there are designated no less the Son and the Spirit than the Father . . ." Institutes, I: XIII: 20.

[21] Vide Matt. 11:25, 26; 26:39, 42; Mark 14:36; Luke 10:21; 22:42; 23:34, 46; John 11:41; 12:27, 28; 17:1, 5, 11, 21, 24, 25. The exception, the cry from the cross (Matt. 27:46; Mark 15:34), is a quotation from Psalm 22.

[22] Cf. Matt. 18:19; John 4:21, 23.

[23] Eph. 1:17; 3:14; Col. 1:12; 3:17; I Pet. 1:17, etc.

[24] Joachim Jeremias, The Prayers of Jesus (Naperville, Ill.: Alec R. Allenson, 1967).

[25] Ibid., pp. 54-57.

[26] Ibid., p. 63.

[27] Ibid., p. 65.

[28] Ibid., pp. 62f.

[29] Institutes, III: XX: 37.

[30] Jeremias, op.cit., p. 62.

CHAPTER IV The Role of Jesus Christ in Prayer

[1] Karl Barth names the Lord's Prayer as included in the five "traditionellen Lehrstucken" which form the basis of the Church's teaching. Karl Barth, Die christliche Lehre Nach dem Heidelberger Katechismus (Zurich: Evangelischer Verlag A. G. Zollikon, 1948), p. 18.

[2] Buttrick, op.cit., p. 29.

[3] John Calvin, Commentaries on the Epistle of Paul the Apostle to the Hebrews, trans. by John Owen (Grand Rapids, Mich.: Wm. B. Eerdmans Publishing Company, 1948) p. 122.

[4] Vide Jeremias, op. cit., pp. 66-78, for a discussion of Jesus' practice of prayer against the background of Jewish tradition.

[5] Because Jesus' teaching on prayer is discussed throughout the thesis, no attempt is made to summarize that teaching in a separate section.

[6] F. Godet, Commentary on the Gospel of John, trans. by Timothy Dwight, II (3rd ed.; New York: Fund and Wagnalls, 1886), p. 277.

[7] Idem.

[8] John Calvin, Commentary on the Gospel According to John, trans. by William Pringle, II (Grand Rapids, Mich.: Wm. B. Eerdmans Publishing Company, 1949), p. 153.

[9] E. W. Hengstenberg, Commentary on the Gospel of John, II (Edinburgh: T. and T. Clark, 1865), p. 299.

[10] Calvin, Commentary on the Gospel According to John, II, p. 154.

[11] For a summary of the revelation contained in the "name" of Christ, vide TDNT, V, pp. 272ff.

[12] Cf. Acts 7:56, Rom. 8:34.

[13] Here the analogy with Esther's approach to Ahasuerus breaks down.

[14] " . . . he who has *parrēsia* need not be ashamed before the coming Judge, will not be put to shame by Him, and has no fear of punishment." TDNT, V, p. 882.

[15] Significantly, Paul links *parrēsia* with *prosagōgē* in Eph. 3:12—the subjective confidence accompanies the objective right of access to God.

[16] John Murray, The Heavenly Priestly Activity of Christ

(London: Westminster Chapel, 1958), p. 9.

[17] Heb. 4:14- 10:25.

[18] In Hebrews, with one exception, the plural of *to hagion* de-notes the Holy of Holies. Vide Heb. 8:2; 9:8, 12, 24, 25; 13:11. The exception is Heb. 9:2, 3, where *hagia* denotes the Holy Place, while the Holy of Holies is called *hagia hagiōn.*

[19] Franz Delitzsch, Commentary on the Epistle to the He-brews, trans. by Thomas L. Kingsbury, II (Grand Rapids, Mich.: Wm. B. Eerdmans Publishing Company, 1952), p. 170.

[20] "Note that the contrast is not between a new and an old way, but between a new way and no way." Marvin R. Vincent, Word Studies in the New Testament, IV (New York: Charles Scrib-ner's Sons, 1914), p. 500.

[21] "No saint of the Old Testament, in whatever degree he might stand of preparatory or prevenient grace, could . . . draw nigh to God so confidently, so joyously, so familiarly as we can now." Delitzsch, op.cit., p. 171.

[22] Calvin, Commentaries on the Epistle of Paul the Apostle to the Hebrews, p. 235.

[23] Calvin, Commentary on the Gospel According to John, II, p. 158.

[24] Murray, op.cit., p. 13.

[25] Supra, pp. 25f.

[26] Murray, loc. cit.

[27] The Holy Spirit is sent in answer to the prayer of the Son (John 14:16); and the Spirit enables Christians to pray. Vide chap. V.

[28] TDNT, III, pp. 301ff.

CHAPTER V   The Work of the Holy Spirit in Prayer

[1] Translators no doubt regard *pneuma douleias* as a servile disposition, rather than the Holy Spirit, because "Spirit of bondage" seems an inappropriate designation for the Holy Spirit. But, in John Murray's view, "The solution resides in the consideration that the proposition respecting the 'Spirit of bondage' is negative and there is no reason why we should not interpret the thought to be, 'Ye did not receive the Holy Spirit as a Spirit of bondage but as the Spirit of adoption.' " John Murray, The Epistle to the Romans, I (Grand Rapids, Mich.: Wm. B. Eerdmans Publishing Company, [1959], pp. 296f.

[2] Ibid., p. 296.

³ Supra, pp. 44ff.

⁴ TDNT, III, pp. 898ff.

⁵ Ibid., p. 903.

⁶ The RSV makes the manner of prayer to be faulty; but the Greek indicates that it is the content of prayer which is the problem —not how (pōs) but what (ti) to pray.

⁷ John Calvin, Commentaries on the Epistle of Paul the Apostle to the Romans, trans. and ed. by John Owen (Grand Rapids, Mich.; Wm. B. Eerdmans Publishing Company, 1947), p. 312.

⁸ Abraham Kuyper, The Work of the Holy Spirit, p. 639.

⁹ A. T. Robertson, A Grammar of the Greek New Testament in the Light of Historical Research (2nd ed.; New York: Hodder and Stoughton, [1919]), p. 573.

¹⁰ Charles Hodge notes that entugchanō, in its derivative sense, means "to intercede for." But then he makes this the equivalent of " . . . to act the part of advocate in behalf of any one." Thus, he sees the action of the Spirit described in this passage as similar to that which " . . . it was the special duty of the advocate to perform, i.e., to dictate to his clients what they ought to say, how they should present their cause." Charles Hodge, A Commentary on the Epistle to the Romans (New York: Hodder and Stoughton, [1882]), p. 438. But entugchanō does not mean "to advise"; the function of the paraklētos was principally to intercede for the accused, not to advise him. Cf. TDNT, V, pp. 800ff.

¹¹ It is unlikely that the stenagmois alalētois might include speaking in tongues, as Kuyper suggests (The Work of the Holy Spirit, p. 637). For alalētois does not signify a lack of intelligible speech, but the failure of speech itself. Cf. Trench, op.cit., pp. 286ff.

¹² Cf. Charles Hodge, A Commentary on the Epistle to the Romans, p. 439.

¹³ Kuyper, The Work of the Holy Spirit, p. 639.

¹⁴ Murray, The Epistle to the Romans, I, p. 313.

¹⁵ Kuyper, The Work of the Holy Spirit, pp. 639f.

CHAPTER VI   Qualifications in the One Who Prays

¹ Institutes, III: XX: 40.

² Heidelberg Catechism, quest. 122; Cochrane, op.cit., p. 329.

³ It is not clear that James 5:16 refers to fervency in prayer. If energoumenē is taken as a middle, the meaning is "The prayer of

a just one has much power when it energizes itself," and this would denote fervor in prayer. But the word may be passive, and then the reference would be to prayer that is energized by the Holy Spirit. Cf. Joseph B. Mayor, The Epistle of St. James (Grand Rapids, Mich.: Zondervan Publishing House, 1954), pp. 177-179.

4 Institutes, III: XX: 6.

5 Ibid., III: XX: 43.

6 Infra, pp. 89ff.

7 The RSV gives the same basic meaning, but is unnecessarily awkward.

8 Vide chap IX.

9 Infra, pp. 86ff.

10 Institutes, III: XX: 10.

11 "Who would break forth into such rashness as to claim for himself the honor of a son of God unless we had been adopted as children of grace in Christ? He, while he is the true Son, has of himself been given us as a brother that what he has of his own by nature may become ours by benefit of adoption if we embrace this great blessing with sure faith." Calvin, Institutes, III: XX: 36.

CHAPTER VII   The Content of Prayer

1 Joachim Jeremias finds in Jesus' use of phrases from the ritual prayers of Judaism an indication that the Saviour's practice of prayer was probably a combination of the repetition of Old Testament forms and the use of free prayer. Jeremias, The Prayers of Jesus, pp. 72-78.

2 The question of the proper content of prayer occurs in connection with all kinds of prayer; but it is most acute in relation to petitionary prayer.

3 A. T. Robertson, Word Pictures in the New Testament, I (New York and London: Harper and Brothers, [1930]), p. 361f.

4 R. C. H. Lenski, The Interpretation of St. Mark's Gospel (Columbus, Ohio: The Wartburg Press, [1946]), p. 495f.

5 G. B. Winer, A Treatise on the Grammar of New Testament Greek, trans. by W. F. Moulton (Edinburgh, T. and T. Clark, 1882), p. 232.

6 Hengstenberg, op.cit., II, pp. 204ff.

7 Ibid., p. 205.

8 Lenski, op.cit., p. 494.

9 The reasoning may be presented in the form of a syllogism:

since God hears prayers that are according to his will, and it is possible to know that one's prayers are heard, then it must be possible to know that one's prayers are according to God's will.

[10] Vide infra, pp. 92f.

[11] Supra, pp. 50ff.

[12] R. C. H. Lenski, The Interpretation of St. John's Gospel (Columbus, Ohio: Lutheran Book Concern, 1942), p. 991.

[13] Institutes, III: XX: 27.

[14] Ibid., III: XX: 48.

[15] The content of proper prayer is being discussed here in terms of its limits, because to attempt to present positively all that should be included in that content would be an almost endless task. The Lord's Prayer has provided the basis for an immense body of literature on the content of prayer. Within the Reformed tradition, classical statements include Calvin's exposition of the Lord's Prayer (Institutes, III: XX: 34-49), quest. 120-129 of the Heidelberg Catechism, quest. 186-196 of the Westminster Larger Catechism, and quest. 99-107 of the Westminster Shorter Catechism.

[16] Institutes, III: XX: 12.

[17] Ibid., III: XX: 15.

[18] Ibid., III: XX: 50.

[19] Kuyper, The Work of the Holy Spirit, pp. 620f.

CHAPTER IX The Defense of Prayer

[1] S. D. Gordon, op.cit., p. 54.

[2] " . . . there are people . . . in that lower, lost world . . . who are there . . . because some one failed to put his life in touch with God, and pray." Ibid., p. 195.

[3] Institutes, III: XX: 3.

[4] John Murray, Calvin on Scripture and Divine Sovereignty (Grand Rapids, Mich.: Baker Book House 1960), p. 70.

[5] Institutes, I: XVII: 3.

[6] Ibid., I: XVII: 4.

[7] " . . . the temptation that constantly besets us is that we wish to comprehend how any activity on the part of man can have meaning. This we can never expect to do because God . . . is incomprehensible to man." Cornelius Van Til, An Introduction to Systematic Theology (unpublished syllabus), p. 28.

[8] Friedrich Heiler, Prayer, trans. and ed. by Samuel McComb (London, New York and Toronto: Oxford University Press, 1933),

p. 362.

[9] Charles Hodge, <u>Systematic Theology</u>, III, pp. 693ff.

[10] George Arthur Buttrick, <u>op.cit.</u>, p. 7.

[11] William Adams Brown, <u>The Life of Prayer in a World of Science</u> (New York: Association Press, 1927). Brown's views are significant because he was a professor (and acting President in 1925) of Union Theological Seminary in New York from 1892 to 1936.

[12] <u>Ibid.</u>, p. 33.

[13] <u>Ibid.</u>, p. 35. (footnote).

[14] <u>Ibid.</u>, pp. 35f.

[15] <u>Ibid.</u>, p. 131.

[16] <u>Ibid.</u>, p. 38.

[17] <u>Ibid.</u>, p. 91.

[18] <u>Ibid.</u>, p. 45.

[19] <u>Ibid.</u>, pp. 133ff.

[20] <u>Ibid.</u>, p. 144.

[21] <u>Ibid.</u>, p. 125.

[22] Brown makes no claim that his view is a Biblical one.

[23] G. C. Berkouwer, <u>The Providence of God</u>, trans. by Lewis Smedes (Grand Rapids, Mich.: Wm. B. Eerdmans Publishing Company, 1952), p. 208.

[24] <u>Ibid.</u>, p. 212. (Quoted from <u>E Voto,</u> I, pp. 238ff.).

[25] P. R. Baelz, <u>Prayer and Providence</u> (London, S.C.M. Press, 1968), p. 7.

[26] John Macquarrie, <u>Principles of Christian Theology</u> (New York: Charles Scribner's Sons, [1966]).

[27] <u>Ibid.</u>, p. ix.

[28] <u>Ibid.</u>, p. 103.

[29] <u>Idem.</u>

[30] <u>Ibid.</u>, p. 94.

[31] <u>Ibid.</u>, p. 437.

[32] <u>Ibid.</u>, p. 438.

[33] <u>Ibid.</u>, p. 439.

[34] <u>Ibid.</u>, p. 439.

[35] <u>Ibid.</u>, p. 440.

[36] Robert L. Simpson, <u>The Interpretation of Prayer in the Early Church</u> (Philadelphia: The Westminster Press, [1965]).

[37] <u>Ibid.</u>, 157.

[38] <u>Ibid.</u>, 161.

[39] Ibid., 162.
[40] Ibid., 157.
[41] Ibid., 162.
[42] Idem.
[43] Ibid., 171.
[44] Ibid., 172.
[45] Ibid., 164ff.

bibliography

Works on Prayer

Baelz, P.R., Prayer and Providence, London: S.C.M. Press, 1968.

Barth, Karl, Prayer According to the Catechisms of the Reformation, trans. by Sara F. Terrien, Philadelphia: The Westminster Press, [1952].

Bishop, Selma L., Issac Watts: Hymns and Spiritual Songs 1707-1748, London: The Faith Press, 1962.

Bauman, Edward W., Intercessory Prayer, Philadelphia: The Westminster Press, [1958].

Brown, William Adams, The Life of Prayer in a World of Science, New York: Association Press, 1927.

Buttrick, George Arthur, Prayer, New York and Nashville: Abingdon-Cokesbury Press, [1942].

Forsyth, P.T., The Soul of Prayer, London: Independent Press, 1949.

Gordon, S.D., Quiet Talks on Prayer, New York: Fleming H. Revell Company, [1904].

Heiler, Friedrich, Prayer, trans. by Samuel McComb, London: Oxford University Press, [1932].

Hodge, Charles, Conference Papers, New York: Charles Scribner's Sons, 1879.

Jenkins, Daniel, Prayer and the Service of God, London: Faber and Faber, [1944].

Jeremias, Joachim, The Prayers of Jesus, Naperville, Ill.: Alec R. Allenson, 1967.

Lewis, C.S., Letters to Malcolm: Chiefly on Prayer, New York: Harcourt, Brace and World, [1963].

Nedoncelle, Maurice, The Nature and Use of Prayer, trans. by A. Manson, London: Burns and Oates, [1964].

Ott, Heinrich, "Theologie als Gebet und Wissenschaft," Theologische Zeitschrift, XIV (1958), 120-132.

Ott, Wilhelm, Gebet und Heil, Munchen: Kosel-Verlag, 1965.

Owen, John, "A Discourse of the Work of the Holy Spirit in Prayer," The Works of John Owen, ed. by William Goold, vol. IV, London and Edinburgh: Johnstone and Hunter, 1852.

Simpson, Robert L., The Interpretation of Prayer in the Early
    Church, Philadelphia: The Westminster Press, [1965].
                    Theological Works
Barth, Karl, Die christliche Lehre nach dem Heidelberger Katechis-
    mus, Zurich: Evangelischer A. G. Zollikon, 1948.
_____., Church Dogmatics, vol. III, part 3, ed. by G. W. Bromiley
    and T. F. Torrance, trans. by G. W. Bromiley and R. J. Ehrlich,
    Edinburgh, T. and T. Clark, [1960].
Berkouwer, G. C., The Providence of God, trans. by Lewis Smedes,
    Grand Rapids, Mich.: Wm. B. Eerdmans Publishing Company,
    1952.
Calvin, John, Institutes of the Christian Religion, 2 vols. (vols. XX
    and XXI of The Library of Christian Classics), ed. by John T.
    McNeill, trans. by Ford Lewis Battles, Philadelphia: The West-
    minster Press, [1960].
Dick, John, Lectures on Theology, vol. II, New York: Robert Car-
    ter and Brothers, 1868.
Fairbairn, Patrick, The Typology of Scripture, vol. I, Philadelphia:
    Daniels & Smith, 1852.
Heppe, Heinrich, Reformed Dogmatics, trans. by G. T. Thomson,
    London: George Allen and Unwin, 1950.
Hodge, Charles, Systematic Theology, vol. III, Grand Rapids, Mich.:
    Wm. B. Eerdmans Publishing Company, 1952.
Kuyper, Abraham, Principles of Sacred Theology, trans. by J.
    Hendrik de Vries, Grand Rapids, Mich.: Wm. B. Eerdmans
    Publishing Company, 1965.
_____., The Work of the Holy Spirit, trans. by Henri de Vries, New
    York and London: Funk and Wagnalls Company, [1900].
Macquarrie, John, Principles of Christian Theology, New York:
    Charles Scribner's Sons, [1966].
Murray, John, Calvin on Scripture and Divine Sovereignty, Grand
    Rapids, Mich.: Baker Book House, 1960.
Murray, John, The Heavenly Priestly Activity of Christ, London:
    Westminster Chapel, 1958.
Pieper, Francis, Christian Dogmatics, vol. III, Saint Louis, Mo.:
    Concordia Publishing House, 1953.
Strong, A. H., Systematic Theology, vol. II, Philadelphia: Griffith
    and Rowland Press, [1907].
Van Til, Cornelius, "An Introduction to Systematic Theology"
    (unpublished syllabus).

Commentaries

Calvin, John, Commentary on a Harmony of the Evangelists, Matthew, Mark, and Luke, trans. by William Pringle, vol. III, Grand Rapids, Mich.: Wm. B. Eerdmans Publishing Company, 1948.

_____., Commentaries on the Epistle of Paul the Apostle to the Hebrews, trans. by John Owen, Grand Rapids, Mich.: Wm. B. Eerdmans Publishing Company, 1948.

_____., Commentary on the Gospel According to John, trans. by William Pringle, vol. II, Grand Rapids, Mich.: Wm. B. Eerdmans Publishing Company, 1949.

_____., Commentaries on the Epistle of Paul the Apostle to the Romans, trans. and ed. by John Owen, Grand Rapids, Mich.: Wm. B. Eerdmans Publishing Company, 1947.

Delitzsch, Franz, Commentary on the Epistle to the Hebrews, trans. by Thomas L. Kingsbury, 2 vols., Grand Rapids, Mich.: Wm. B. Eerdmans Publishing Company, 1952.

Godet, F., Commentary on the Gospel of John, trans. by Timothy Dwight, 3rd ed., vol. II, New York: Fund and Wagnalls, 1886.

Hengstenberg, E. W., Commentary on the Gospel of John, vol. II, Edinburgh: T. and T. Clark, 1865.

Hodge, Charles, A Commentary on the Epistle to the Romans, New York: Hodder and Stoughton, [1882].

Lenski, R. C. H., The Interpretation of the Epistle to the Hebrews and of the Epistle of James, Columbus, Ohio: The Wartburg Press, [1946].

_____., The Interpretation of St. John's Gospel, Columbus, Ohio: Lutheran Book Concern, [1942].

Lenski, R. C. H., The Interpretation of St. Mark's Gospel, Columbus, Ohio: The Wartburg Press, [1946].

_____., The Interpretation of St. Matthew's Gospel, Columbus, Ohio: The Wartburg Press, [1943].

_____., The Interpretation of St. Paul's Epistle to the Romans, Columbus, Ohio: The Wartburg Press, [1945].

Mayor, Joseph B., The Epistle of St. James, Grand Rapids, Mich.: Zondervan Publishing House, 1954.

Murray, John, The Epistle to the Romans, vol. I, Grand Rapids, Mich.: Wm. B. Eerdmans Publishing Company, [1959].

Owen, John, An Exposition of the Epistle to the Hebrews, vol. IV, Edinburgh, 1813.

Robertson, A. T., Word Pictures in the New Testament, Vol. I, New

York and London: Harper and Brothers, [1930].

Vincent, Marvin R., Word Studies in the New Testament, vol. IV, New York: Charles Scribner's Sons, 1914.

Reference Works

The Catholic Encyclopedia, vol. II, New York: Robert Appleton Company, [1907].

The Constitution of the Reformed Presbyterian Church of North America, Pittsburgh, Pa.: The Synod of the Reformed Presbyterian Church, 1949.

The Theological Dictionary of the New Testament, ed. by Gerhard Kittel, trans. and ed. by G. W. Bromiley, vols. II, III, V, Grand Rapids, Mich.: Wm. B. Eerdmans Publishing Company, [1964, 1965, 1967].

Liddell, Henry George, and Scott, Robert, A Greek-English Lexicon, 2 vols., Oxford; The Clarendon Press, 1940.

Moulton, James Hope, and Milligan, George, The Vocabulary of the Greek Testament, London: Hodder and Stoughton, 1952.

Reformed Confessions of the 16th Century, ed. by Arthur C. Cochrane, Philadelphia: The Westminster Press, [1966].

Robertson, A. T., A Grammar of the Greek New Testament in the Light of Historical Research, 2nd ed., New York: Hodder and Stoughton, [1919].

Schroeder, H. J., Canons and Decrees of the Council of Trent, St. Louis, Mo. and London: B. Herder Book Company, 1941.

Trench, R. C., Synonyms of the New Testament, 12th ed., London: Kegan Paul, Trench, Trubner and Company, 1894.

Winer, G. B., A Treatise on the Grammar of New Testament Greek, trans. by W. F. Moulton, Edinburgh: T. and T. Clark, 1882.

appendix

the location of prayer in the encyclopedia of theology

The Location of Prayer In the Encyclopedia of Theology

Reformed theologians have followed three courses with regard to the theological discussion of prayer. Some have failed to give any separate treatment to prayer at all, dealing with it only in so far as questions about prayer arise in connection with other topics of theology, such as the doctrine of providence. Others have listed prayer as a means of grace, along with the Word and the Sacraments. Others have placed the discussion under the heading of the doctrine of sancitification or of the Christian life. The third alternative is to be preferred, for the following reasons:

1.   Since prayer occupies so important a place in the life of the individual Christian and of the Church, and since historically it has been one of the main divisions of instruction in the faith, systematic theology cannot afford to give it only fragmentary consideration. Belief and practice come together in an intimate way in prayer, so that erroneous thinking concerning prayer very directly affects an individual's (or the Church's) relationship with God. It is not enough that special problems concerning prayer should be discussed at various points within the system of doctrine. Just as it is important to deal with the doctrine of God systematically, in order to achieve as comprehensive and consistent an understanding as possible, so the teaching of Scripture concerning prayer must be drawn together to form a balanced and coherent doctrine of prayer.

2.   It is inappropriate to treat prayer as one of the means of grace, because whereas the Word and Sacraments (and church discipline) are objectively given, external means by which God conveys his mercy, prayer is the subjective response to God's grace. Of course, God's mercy is given in answer to prayer (Heb. 4:16), and in that sense it is a means by which grace is obtained from God. But prayer remains fundamentally the activity of a man toward God, while the Word and Sacrament are means of grace in the technical sense, in that they represent God's activity towards man. With regard to the Word and Sacraments, the believer is primarily receptive; in prayer he is primarily active. (Vide Francis Pieper, Christian

Dogmatics, III (St. Louis, Missouri: Concordia Publishing House, 1953), p. 215 for a discussion of this point from a Lutheran standpoint).

3.　Since prayer is the activity of a person who has received the grace of God, the theological discussion of it clearly belongs in the area of soteriology. Since prayer is a continuing response to God's grace, it is closely connected with the process of sanctification. There are a number of ways in which sanctification can be dealt with systematically; but whatever method is adopted, prayer ought to be a topic for discussion as a part of sanctification. (Calvin's organization in the Institutes of the Christian Religion regards prayer as the primary expression of faith in Bk. III, while the preaching of the Word, church discipline, and the Sacraments are treated under the doctrine of the Church, in Bk. IV.)